Three cheers! Lee Jenkins accomplishes something imp[ortant] [in a book of] this sort. He weds solid Christian teaching to financial practices and places fascinating dialogue within the context of African American history and culture. With the voice and heart of a master teacher, he clearly sets forth the ABC's of financial literacy.

> Dr Robert M. Franklin, President
> Interdenominational Theological Center
> Atlanta, GA

Taking Care of Business is the financial answer to keeping our families strong. Lee Jenkins has produced a practical guide, using Christian principles that will help families become financially savvy.

> Judge Glenda Hatchett
> The Judge Hatchett Show

Taking Care of Business is long overdue. It is one of the most relevant and challenging books I have read recently. In this book, Lee covers the ABC's of finances and business in general. There is no doubt that this best seller will better the lives of individuals, families, churches and communities. Lee's personal integrity, vision, and passion position him to speak with authority.

> Dr. Samuel R. Chand, President
> Beulah Heights Bible College
> Atlanta, GA

What a blessing! My good friend Lee Jenkins has put together a remarkable book. It is biblically sound, culturally relevant, practical, easy to understand, and hard-hitting.

> Minister Reggie White
> Former NFL Superstar

Lee Jenkins is uniquely qualified to be heard. I believe he is undoubtedly the right man for this kind of project. In his new book *Taking Care of Business* Lee draws from his abundant wisdom as a stellar financial advisor and his extensive ministry experience. I highly recommend this book.

> Howard Dayton
> Co-CEO Crown Financial Ministries

Every decade a great stewardship book is called forward from an insightful leader . . . a leader who knows the financial pulse of the issues of the day for families, the church, and parachurch ministries. For such a time as this, this is that book and Jenkins is that leader. Buy a copy for anyone you consdier dear in your life.

> Scott Preissler, M.Ed., M.A., President
> Christian Stewardship Association

The Negro National Anthem

Lift every voice and sing
Till earth and heaven ring,
Ring with the harmonies of Liberty;
Let our rejoicing rise
High as the listening skies,
Let it resound loud as the rolling sea.
Sing a song full of the faith that the dark past has taught us,
Sing a song full of the hope that the present has brought us,
Facing the rising sun of our new day begun
Let us march on till victory is won.

So begins the Black National Anthem, by James Weldon Johnson in 1900. Lift Every Voice is the name of the joint imprint of The Institute for Black Family Development and Moody Press, a division of the Moody Bible Institute.

Our vision is to advance the cause of Christ through publishing African-American Christians who educate, edify, and disciple Christians in the church community through quality books written for African-Americans.

The Institute for Black Family Development is a national Christian organization. It offers degreed and nondegreed training nationally and internationally to established and emerging leaders from churches and Christian organizations. To learn more about The Institute for Black Family Development write us at:

The Institute for Black Family Development
15151 Faust
Detroit, Michigan 48223

Moody Press, a ministry of Moody Bible Institute,
is designed for education, evangelization, and edification.
If we may assist you in knowing more about Christ
and the Christian life, please write us without obligation:

Moody Press
c/o Moody Literature Ministries
820 N. LaSalle Blvd.
Chicago, Illinois 60610.

Taking Care of
BUSINESS

ESTABLISHING A
FINANCIAL LEGACY
FOR THE AFRICAN
AMERICAN FAMILY

LEE JENKINS

MOODY PRESS
CHICAGO

All Scripture quotations, unless otherwise indicated, are taken from the *New American Standard Bible®*, © Copyright The Lockman Foundation 1960, 1962, 1963, 1968, 1971, 1972, 1973, 1975, 1977, 1995. Used by permission.

Scripture quotations marked TLB are taken from *The Living Bible* copyright © 1971. Used by permission of Tyndale House Publishers, Inc., Wheaton, Illinois 60189. All rights reserved.

Scripture quotations marked NIV are taken from the *Holy Bible, New International Version®*. NIV®. Copyright © 1973, 1978, 1984 by International Bible Society. Used by permission of Zondervan Publishing House. All rights reserved.

Scripture quotations marked AMP are taken from *The Amplified Bible.* Copyright © 1965, 1987 by The Zondervan Corporation. The Amplified New Testament copyright © 1958, 1987 by The Lockman Foundation. Used by permission.

Scripture quotations marked KJV are taken from the King James Version.

Library of Congress Cataloging-in-Publication Data

Jenkins, Lee, 1961-
   Taking care of business : establishing a financial legacy for the african-american family / Lee Jenkins.
      p. cm.
   Includes bibliographical references.
   ISBN 0-8024-4016-9
   1. Finance, Personal—Religious aspects—Christianity. 2. African Americans—Finance, Personal. I. Title.

HG179 .J368 2001
332.024—dc21

                                                    2001044150

1 3 5 7 9 10 8 6 4 2

Printed in the United States of America

To My Parents
Mrs. Alfreda I. Jenkins & The late Lee A. Jenkins, Sr.
THANKS FOR TRAINING ME IN THE WAY I SHOULD GO

CONTENTS

FOREWORD

My good friend Lee Jenkins is one among a growing number of African-American Christian authors who have developed an expertise that is of inestimable value to the black community in particular, as well as to the body of Christ at large. As a successful businessman in the area of financial planning, Lee has successfully married the biblical concepts of technical excellence and spiritual maturity to the area of handling money.

In this groundbreaking work, Lee clearly articulates God's view of money in practical everyday speech that will educate and inspire the reader to bring this sensitive area of life under the lordship of Jesus Christ. Lee demonstrates that how we win and handle mammon is a good indicator of our spiritual temperature.

A work such as this is particularly needed in the African-American church where the emphasis has historically been on the biblical injunctions regarding giving rather than the broader teaching on money management. Lee covers all the major bases relative to money leaving the reader both educated and motivated to make the necessary adjustments in their lives to begin experiencing God's plan for their lives in the area of finances.

Because of Lee's strong Christian faith that pervades this work, the reader will not only become wealthier in this world's goods, but will also reap an abundance of spiritual wealth as well. Furthermore, because Lee interjects many of his own life experiences in this book, the reader will be kept from the curse of lifeless instruction. This book pulsates with the life of a man who knows his God, and who desires to help people. This combination makes for a book that will not only inform but also transform.

The Kingdom of God is in great need of men of integrity who both know their fields as well as know their God. Lee Jenkins is such a man, and when you have finished reading this book you will be able to begin the process of moving from economic bondage to economic freedom, not only for yourself but your family, your church, and even the next generation. You will be much more prepared to begin taking care of business.

DR. TONY EVANS

FOREWORD

When I first encountered Lee Jenkins, I could tell he was a man on a mission. I was especially impressed with his deep commitment to God that touched everyone he met with love and the overwhelming desire to set them free financially. He was like a John the Baptist, the voice of one crying in the wilderness. That voice was the one voice never really heard to the fullest in our community at large: the voice of financial freedom and empowerment. Finally, Lee Jenkins, in his prophetic treatise *Taking Care of Business,* is a voice of financial emancipation. He gives us a picture of the ultimate plan of God. For a people who cannot see the ultimate, they become a slave to the immediate. The immediate is the world system and poverty is its end. The book you hold in your hand is filled with simple, biblical truths about finances and how to obtain and sustain wealth with godly integrity. Walking in what is revealed develops a total biblical character in you and your family. Using his own life experiences along with others, he explores the path of economic growth within the black experience in America to a kingdom view of empowerment. I believe the Lord called for this book for such a time as now, to radically change your financial status and destroy the spirit of poverty over you, and to permanently set free generations yet born. This book will challenge you to grow and prosper. As you read and study this great writing, allow each page to come to life. In doing so, you will establish a legacy for you and your family.

BISHOP EDDIE L. LONG, D.D., D.H.L.
Senior Pastor, New Birth Missionary Baptist Church

ACKNOWLEDGMENTS

To my Wife, Martica: You are the love of my life. You bring out the best in me. Thanks for your support and for being my biggest cheerleader. You are truly a blessing from God!

To my Children, Kristin, Martin & Ryan: My three bundles of joy! I'm blessed to be your Dad.

To my Sister, Sonya T. Jenkins: You always believed in me and I in you. Let's make Mom and Dad proud!

To Howard Dayton: You were the first person to encourage me to write a book. I am forever indebted to you and The Crown Financial Ministries family for the impact made on my life. Thank you so much for your friendship. Also, I appreciate your letting me borrow some of your materials from your book; *Your Money Counts.*

To Dr. Tony Evans: Your preaching and teaching has always been a blessing to my life, but getting to know you as a friend has been even better! Thanks for writing the foreword.

To Bishop Eddie Long: Every time I leave your presence I feel inspired. You are a great leader. Thanks for writing the foreword.

The Pastors & Ministry Leaders who have impacted my life: Every one of you has influenced my life in a special way. Thank you so much for investing a part of your life in me.

> Rev. O. L. Blackshear
> Brother Billy McCool
> Sam Mings
> Bishop Flynn & Carolyn Johnson
> Rev. A. J. McMichael
> Pastor Marvin Winans
> Crawford Loritts
> Bishop Keith Butler
> Pastor Jamie Pleasant
> Pastors Bill & D'Ann Johnson
> Pastor Bryan Crute
> Ron Blue

To All of my friends, especially Keenan Nix, Terry Lucas, & Kelvin Phillips: Your friendship, prayers, and encouragement regarding this project were invaluable to me. Thanks so much.

To Walt Walker & Steve Wamburg: Your help and encouragement early on in this project was sincerely appreciated. You guys told me I could do it, and here it is!

To Cynthia Ballenger, Greg Thornton, and the rest of the Moody Press family: Thanks for believing in my message and me.

To my Lord and Savior Jesus Christ: All that I am and ever hope to be, I owe it all to thee.

Introduction

BIGGER AND BETTER DREAMS

I was quickly ushered out of the administrative offices of the New York Giants into the limo waiting to take me to the airport. When you get cut from the National Football League, you are called to the office and told to bring your playbook. That's when you know it's all over. I was cut because of an injury, and since I couldn't pass the medical exam, no other team would be interested. Like anyone would be, I was disappointed to suddenly learn that my lifelong dream of fame and fortune in the NFL was over. There would be no six-figure salary, TV commercials, or endorsements for me. No Mercedes Benz and big house and expensive stylish clothes. Incidentally, I was accompanied in the limo by a couple of three-hundred-pound offensive linemen who had also been cut. It was quite a sight to see these two big guys sitting there crying like babies. Like those two great big guys, my dream of NFL stardom had come and gone.

I came into the NFL with no money; then over a short period of time, I made a lot of it; but in the end, I had no idea what had happened to it. Being sent back to the real world where I had to find a real job and make a career for myself was a financial wake-up call. For me that meant shifting gears, starting all over, and looking for a new dream to pursue.

However, it was, as they say, the first day of the rest of my life. It signaled the beginning of a spiritual journey on which I would learn the principles that would mark my life, my career, and my financial success more than I could have ever imagined. It answered a question I didn't even know to ask—How does one handle money God's way? I had been taught from childhood about the life-transforming power of the Bible, and in college I had personally had a dramatic spiritual encounter with Christ. Though I had also heard about tithing (giving 10 percent to God), it had never occurred to me that there were clear and straightforward principles in Scripture concerning how we managed the other 90 percent.

FAITH, FINANCES, AND THE BLACK CHURCH

The role of faith—almost exclusively the Christian faith—cannot be overestimated in the relation of the Black experience. It is undeniably one of the core dimensions in the life of most Blacks in America, regardless of age, gender, or education. The Black church has always been the single most important institution in the African-American community. Next to the extended family, it is the oldest continuous Black institution and one that has been at the forefront of addressing both spiritual and social needs. Every Sunday morning twenty-one million worshipers attend more than 43,000 predominately Black churches in America. Though these churches share the same fundamental beliefs and practices as other Christian churches, there are distinctions far greater than color that have caused our congregations to be completely unique.

Like many of the early Christian churches, the African-American church was born in the midst of unimaginable oppression, and even today it bears the mark of those beginnings. The Black church's beginning was bitter, forged in the crucible of slavery. Scholars estimate that the first Black churches were created in the 1790s when slaves left the segregated pews of White churches to form their own houses of worship. These first Black churches offered a brief refuge from slavery, a place where enslaved Blacks could throw themselves fully into the worship experience by shouting, stomping, weeping, even collapsing on the floor. Many of them dreaded working in the fields, so worship was a way to escape the harsh realities of slavery.

Even after slavery, the Black church provided a sense of community and an atmosphere where we could celebrate our uniqueness and be affirmed and accepted as we were. People who were not recognized in the larger society could receive status and recognition in the church. A janitor could become a deacon, a domestic could become head of the usher board, and the Black clergy, almost by default, became the leaders in the community and were expected to speak out on issues of the day. Even the civil rights movement was made possible because of the Black church. The Black church provided spiritual resources, leadership, and places to meet. For most Black churches, the mission was both sacred and secular, and there was no distinction between transforming lives and society.

Economically speaking, the Black church is and has always been the most economically independent institution in the Black community. It does not depend upon White trustees to raise funds, for example, as do most Black colleges. Nor does it depend on White patronage to pay its pastors or erect its buildings.[1] The Black church has also never been dependent on the government. One of the greatest examples of biblical stewardship this country has ever seen was the Black church under slavery. There were no government or social support systems, no federal grants, no welfare systems. Yet without any of that, our ancestors not only carved out a religious order but also banks, legal firms, family support systems, surrogate parenting, and social movements. All of this was done without any government support.

Another distinction of the African-American church has been the catalyst for social and political change. From the abolitionist movement to the present day, every significant advancement for African-Americans has come from or through our churches. Not that the business, government, or other parts of the nonprofit sectors have not contributed, but the mandate and the marching orders to go out and change our situation have originated from the African-American pulpit and from the Bible.

Why then should it be any different for us when it comes to money, finances, and economics? If you come to the church as your refuge, the place that cleanses your soul, then that ought to be the place where you get your financial instruction as well. A 1999 study conducted by the Barna Research Group showed some amazing things about the African-American church. While four hundred Black senior pastors ranked "helping people in crisis" as the greatest ministry priority among twelve categories, they also ranked economic guidance eleventh among twelve categories. Economic guidance was also second to last among their roles in the church. Those statistics reveal the overall position of the church. While Blacks have gotten our instructions and directions for cultural change from the church or the Bible, we have been content to let the world tell us how to handle our financial life. Regardless of your skin color, if you follow the popular advice of the world, you'll wind up in financial bondage. I've seen it happen to so many people, and it's not because people have sat down and decided to mortgage themselves into slavery. Usually, it is because they've just sailed along with the prevailing wind of a consumer society that is being fueled and driven by consumer debt.

STRUGGLING WITH GOD'S ECONOMY

Two economic systems operate in this world—God's economy and the world's economy. It shouldn't surprise us that some people have a hard time thinking of God as being involved in their finances. The Bible says, "'My thoughts are not your thoughts, neither are your ways my ways,' declares the LORD" (Isaiah 55:8 NIV). People usually live by what they can touch and see. Now when I talk about God's being involved with our finances, I don't mean He's going to send an angel with a briefcase full of money, deliver an anonymous check in the mail, or bless you with the right lottery numbers. Now I know that prayer works miracles, but so does the discipline of cutting up your credit cards. God works in our lives in such a way that we don't see Him, we do see His results. Some people think, *Yeah, He's been a little too invisible to me. I need God to show up.* However, the reason God is not playing a more significant role in their finances is that they have been handling money in sharp contrast to God's financial principles.

Jesus lived in a much simpler society than ours. He never had to struggle with a credit card, and never had to deal with the temptations of those easy monthly payments leading to debt. Nevertheless, the Lord Jesus Christ said more about money and material possessions than almost any other subject. It may surprise you to learn just how much the Bible says about finances. There are approximately 500 verses on prayer, fewer than 500 on faith, and more than 2,350 verses on how to handle money and possessions. There are at least three reasons why it was a constant theme in Jesus' teaching.

1. Our possessions can compete with Jesus Christ for first place in our lives.

Money is such a formidable competitor with Jesus Christ for our affections. So much so, that Jesus calls money a master. Jesus knew that either you better master money, or money will master you. That is true whether you are rich, poor, or anywhere in between. Some people get so caught up with what they wish they had that they become more materialistic than those people who actually have it. There are probably just as many poor people guilty of covetousness and materialism as there are rich people. The question is this: What is the relationship between money and God in our lives? To some the cost of discipleship was to make restitution, to others it was to forgive, and still to others it was to go and sin no more. Jesus zeroed in on the idols in a person's life.

Money and possessions as idolatry? Come on now. Who actually bows down and worships money? Consider what the apostle Paul wrote: "Consider the members of your earthly body as dead to immorality, impurity, passion, evil desire, and greed, which amounts to idolatry" (Colossians 3:5). If the Greeks idolized wisdom, the Epicureans idolized pleasure, and the Nazis idolized German nationalism, what do you think

Americans idolize? It is materialism and affluence. Whenever we esteem something other than Christ and His eternal kingdom to be the greatest importance and highest priority in our lives, we've got a problem with idolatry. Jesus always zeroed in on the idols in a person's life.

2. How we handle money impacts our fellowship with the Lord.

This is clearly illustrated in the parable of the talents. The master congratulates the servant who had managed money faithfully by saying, "Well done, good and faithful servant! You have been faithful with a few things; I will put you in charge of many things. Come and share your master's happiness!" (Matthew 25:21 NIV).

People pray a lot about money, but usually it is to ask for help when they have run out of it. Others cry out for divine wisdom and guidance, but only when filling out the number on their lottery ticket. Everyone gets really spiritual when it comes to believing miraculous wealth will appear. But when it comes to managing the money with which they have already been entrusted, they totally disconnect from God in order to manage it their own way.

Discovering that the Bible has so much to say about handling money did three things for me. First of all, it provided the wisdom and spiritual principles to help me be a good and faithful steward. Second, I found out that when you consistently obey God's financial principles, you will begin to see His hand of blessing. Third, as I began to learn what the Bible had to say about handling money, it became clear to me that the way I managed my money and possessions was an essential part of following Jesus Christ. As I began to put biblical principles into practice and recognize that God was the master of my finances, not only did I begin to experience His presence at work, but I could feel I was coming to know God in a new way and that I was sharing in my Master's happiness. What a contrast that was to the past when my attitude, my actions, and especially my anxiety over money tended to hurt my relationship with the Lord. It may surprise you as it did me that the amount of money we have does not affect our lives as much as how we handle what money we have.

3. A large part of our lives revolves around the use of money.

The Lord talked so much about money because He knew that much of our lives would center on its use. What are the things you've been praying about and hoping for lately? On several occasions while speaking in a church, I have asked the question: "How many of your top three prayer requests involve money?" In each case, almost every hand has gone up. You see, money impacts our family life, our social life, our church life, how we look, how we feel about ourselves, and how people feel about God. It is so entwined in our lives there is no way to avoid it.

As our church, through small groups, began to teach what the Bible has to say about handling money, we saw the most dramatic effects. As a result of learning and implementing biblical principles relating to money, African-American families in our church who had struggled financially for generations were typically seeing four things happen: 1) people who had never thought it possible were actually becoming debt-free; 2) those same people were beginning to save, invest, and build financial security; 3) at the same time, they were reassessing what was most valuable in life, becoming more spiritually focused, and learning to put God in the center of everything they did; and 4) they began to teach and train their children, as well as to provide for them a working model. In doing so, they have begun to create a heritage of financial faithfulness and financial security that will be carried on for many generations.

There are a lot of people in the African-American community with financial problems, and I'm not just talking about those with low incomes. In fact, most of those I know who are in deep trouble or who are headed in that direction are those with upper-middle-class incomes, who look like they've "got it going on," who drive BMWs, live in the suburbs, and wear designer clothing.

It doesn't matter who you are. No one is so rich that he doesn't need to learn to manage money God's way. Your height and the color of your eyes are permanent conditions, but your current financial situation is not. The problem is that too many people are looking for ways to get rich without being good stewards and without looking to what the Bible has to say about handling money. No matter how bad or bleak your financial situation presently may be, God is able to do remarkable things in your life and with your finances, but only when you begin to do things His way. Jeremiah 29:11(NIV) states, "'For I know the plans I have for you,'" declares the LORD, 'plans to prosper you and not to harm you, plans to give you hope and a future.'"

A BIBLICAL BASIS FOR
FINANCIAL FAITHFULNESS: MY DREAM

Making it to the NFL was a significant accomplishment. Learning about biblical principles of handling money and becoming a financially successful businessman was even better. However, a greater and much more important dream was being formed in me as I continued to see the lives of people in our church changed both spiritually and financially. Here's my dream:

1. The African-American community in America will emerge from three hundred years of continuing economic bondage by creating a culture of financial faithfulness that we pass on from generation to generation.
2. By learning to handle money according to the principles of Scripture, we as individual families in the African-American community will build a reservoir of capital and financial security. Can African-American kids climb up from poverty to financial security? I believe they can, but it is a very steep and high mountain. Because there is little or no economic capital passed down from generation to generation, many Black kids start at the very bottom of the mountain, and a smaller percentage make it to the top. As African-American families develop the habit of saving for the next generation, it's like building a base camp that makes climbing to the summit a realistic possibility for their children.
3. We will not diminish that which is most important to us. We will refortify our families, our churches, and deepen our spiritual commitments.

The dream would be hard to believe if I hadn't seen it happen in the lives of so many people who have decided to implement the principles from God's Word. In the following pages, I share some of the biblical principles that have so affected my wife, Martica, and myself, as well as so many of our friends. We're convinced that teaching these lessons to our children and grandchildren will be one of the greatest gifts we could ever give them. Our prayer and sincere hope is that your life will be affected as greatly as ours has been. Let's take care of business.

Chapter One

WEALTH FROM THE INSIDE OUT

$\mathcal{A}$ few years ago, an attorney friend asked me to meet with a client of his that had won $3 million playing the lottery two years earlier. The attorney was concerned that the lady was spending too much of her winnings and just needed someone like me to come and talk to her about the importance of saving and investing. The attorney told me that this lady was a committed Christian and that while she was praying two years ago, God gave her the winning lottery numbers. Those particular numbers that she said God had given her led to her $3 million windfall. I must admit I was pretty skeptical about the God-lottery story, but according to the attorney, he thought the lady still had about $500,000 left, and he didn't want her to blow the rest of it on cars, clothes, and greedy family members. I felt it was definitely worth my time to go talk to the lady and make her a client, even though I didn't agree with her theology.

When I met the lady, she was very reserved and withdrawn. As we began to get acquainted, my curiosity got the best of me, so I asked her, "Is it true that you said God gave you the winning lottery numbers?" She got very quiet, and I could tell she was very uncomfortable with that question. She then said, "Yes, that's what I thought back then, but now I know that wasn't true." Then she began to cry uncontrollably. She said, "Lee, I thought that God gave me those numbers, but now, two years later, I know it was the devil!" She told me how miserable her life had been since she won the lottery. She said the money led to a divorce and a strained relationship among her and all of her family members. She said she had to move to Atlanta to get away from them. She went on to say, "I have no friends, and my daughter and I live a miserable life. I bought a huge house and luxury cars, and I'm still unhappy. I was happier when I was making $20,000 a year working at a hospital."

I prayed for her, and she seemed to calm down. Then I figured it was time to get down to business. I asked her how much out of the $3 million she had left. I was shocked at her answer. "Lee, I don't have anything left. I'm broke. I've spent it all up. I need to borrow against my house and sell cars to get some cash so I can live." I asked her how she could spend $3 million in two years when she seemed to live fine off of $20,000 before she won the lottery. She said, "I don't know; I guess that was too much money for a poor person to try to handle."

THE NECESSARY CHANGE:
TAKING THE POVERTY OUT OF PEOPLE

In 1935, President Franklin D. Roosevelt established the New Deal, which set up our current welfare system. A few decades later, in 1964, President Lyndon B. Johnson's War on Poverty was created. Both of these two presidents decided to eliminate poverty by declaring war on it. Since that time the U.S. government has spent a whopping $5 trillion to eliminate poverty—and guess what has happened. The poverty problem in our community still hasn't gone away. As a matter of fact, in some cases it has gotten even worse.

Nearly one out of three Blacks lives in poverty compared with fewer than one in ten Whites. One-third of Black families have no family wealth. Four in ten Black households have less than one thousand dollars in net worth. Single women head two-thirds of Black households, many with low-paying jobs. A generation ago, single parents headed only one-third of Black households. Black unemployment rates are twice those of Whites.[1] Blacks own less than 3 percent of the wealth in America, even though we are 13 percent of the population. Nationally, 30 percent of Black families live below the poverty line, an increase of 20 percent since 1969.[2]

The reason that many people actually became poorer during this time is because money problems can never be solved from the outside in, but only from the inside out. Like the lady who won the lottery, giving someone money who has never been trained to handle it is usually a recipe for disaster. You see, poverty is never corrected by a redistribution of wealth but by a transformation of people. You can give a man begging for food a dollar, but before that day is out he will more than likely be hungry again. Unless there is a change in the person, nothing will change. The government has tried to take people out of poverty. *Jesus specializes in taking the poverty out of people.*

The old saying "Give a man a fish and you feed him for a day; teach a man how to fish and you feed him for a lifetime" is definitely true. Building financial and spiritual wealth that lasts throughout generations starts from the inside. It is a set of choices that become a lifestyle. Unfortunately, so is poverty.

THE WEALTH INSIDE

In Psalm 1:3, David compares the wealthy to a tree. "And he shall be like a tree firmly planted by the streams of water, ready to bring forth his fruit in its season; his leaf also shall not fade or wither, and everything he does shall prosper" (AMP).

I heard a story about a guy who lived in a city that was experiencing a serious drought. Most of the trees in his yard were drying up, and the leaves were turning brown, except for this one beautiful green tree. He called in a tree specialist and was told that the flourishing tree was more than two hundred years old and the roots ran very deep into the ground. As a matter of fact, the roots ran so deep that they connected to channels of water underneath the earth. So no matter how hot or dry it got above the ground, this tree would continuously stay green and healthy and bear much fruit. It was getting fed from underground resources.

In today's economy, wealth is mostly related to money and certain material possessions that we can see, such as land, money, houses, cars, investments, etc. However, in God's economy, true wealth begins with the things that we cannot see. Inward wealth is that special something that God entrusts to each of us. Wealth includes our creative abilities, spiritual knowledge, ideas, character, health, relationships, peace of mind, and contentment. You can have a wealth of ideas, a wealth of knowledge, and a wealth of relationships.

Having money doesn't necessarily mean that you have wealth, though. Some of the poorest people I know have a lot of money. They are poor because they worry about their money all the time. They worry about the stock market; they worry that somebody is always trying to get their money. They worry about their family, their future, and their businesses. Believe me, no matter how much money you have, if you're still worried, you aren't wealthy at all.

Like the tree in Psalm 1, any outward wealth we obtain should be a by-product of our root system. It should be a result of what's going on inside of us. *Wealth is always an inward realization before it is an outward manifestation.* Microsoft was first an idea to Bill Gates before it ever became a billion-dollar company.

That's why so many millionaires can go broke or bankrupt and then, within a few years, bounce back to millionaire status again. It's because wealth is not what they have *on them*, it's what they have *in them*. The external is a by-product of the internal.

Here's an interesting fact: If you took all of the millions of dollars away from the rich and gave it to the poor, within five years you would make an amazing discovery. The rich would have it back again! And what about the poor people—what would happen to them? Most would be flat broke . . . again! In addition, those who were considered poor before receiving the millions might be in even worse condition. They might have even more worries, more family and spending problems than before. Do you know why? *Because wealth is who you are, not just something you have.*

28

THE DIFFERENCE
BETWEEN WEALTH AND RICHES

Did you know that you can be wealthy without having lots of things, or you can be rich and not be wealthy? Although this may sound a little confusing, it is really a crucial point. First of all, we must make a distinction between what we'll call simply riches and wealth. The Bible doesn't distinguish these two by words, but it does by context. Let's look at Psalm 112:1–3 and Ecclesiastes 5:19:

> How blessed is the man who fears the Lord, who greatly delights in His commandments. His descendants will be mighty on earth; the generation of the upright will be blessed. Wealth and riches are in his house, and his righteousness endures forever.

> Furthermore, as for every man to whom God has given riches and wealth, He has also empowered him to eat from them and to receive his reward and rejoice in his labor; this is the gift of God.

Simply stated, "riches" are something we have; "wealth" is something we are. You can become rich with or without God. Think about it— there are many drug dealers, pimps, and crooked businessmen who are rich. You never hear anyone say they struck it wealthy. It is said that they struck it rich. That's because riches are material things; wealth is more spiritual and character-related. Wealth is primarily achieved through the skills, obedience, spiritual knowledge, and character developed in obeying God's laws.

Wealth may produce riches, but riches cannot produce wealth, because wealth comes from obedience to God's covenant.[3] God gives us the power to make wealth. That's why we shouldn't worry about or focus on getting riches, but instead focus on the production of wealth. Matthew 6:33 tells us that we should "seek first His kingdom and His righteousness, and all these things will be added to you." God will take care of the "things" in our lives if we just focus on pleasing Him.

Being in the investment profession, I know quite a few rich people that are very discontent. They are trying to find their satisfaction in riches, but they are never quite content. They are always scratching and clawing for more, only to find that more is still not enough. Why? It's because they are trying to get gratification through riches that is only possible through wealth. Like a man in a lifeboat who in desperation drinks saltwater to quench his thirst, these people find that the more they consume, the more madly they crave.

It is imperative that men and women of God understand this so we won't put the cart before the horse when it comes to material possessions. Having things like a big house and a fancy car should never be the goal in our lives, but a by-product of our faithful stewardship. God is not against our having both wealth and riches. As a matter of fact, many of us need both in order to effectively carry out what God has called us to do and to promote and fund the gospel of the kingdom.

INCOME DOES NOT EQUAL WEALTH

Now let's talk about outward wealth. It's one thing to make a million dollars; it's quite another to be worth a million dollars. In fact, if you worked forty years and earned $2,000 a month, you would have approximately $1 million. Unfortunately, only a tiny fraction of us will ever accumulate a net worth approaching that amount. Why? Because earning money is not the same as retaining wealth.

If Black America were a nation, our income would make us one of the fifteen wealthiest nations in the world. We are thirty-five million strong and control nearly $535 billion in annual income. Within twenty years, our income is estimated to be more than $1 trillion! Now that's tremendous progress, especially taking into account the long history of Black oppression in America. More Blacks are middle class and prosperous than ever before. We have Black CEOs of Fortune 500 corporations, and Blacks are now U.S. senators, governors, Supreme Court justices, United Nations ambassadors, as well as secretary of state. But hold off on the celebration; total income does not translate into wealth.

When I began my career as an investment adviser at the age of twenty-five, I quickly found out that I was not as well off as some of my White colleagues who had the same job title, the same college degree, and the same sized paycheck as I did. We were all around the same age, but they had sizable personal investment portfolios, went on lavish vacations, and were able to afford homes and material things of which I could never dream. I often asked myself, *What am I doing wrong? How can these guys afford to live like this?* One day I struck up a conversation with two of my colleagues, one White, and the other Jewish. We all started in the investment business at the same time and had about the same income. However, they didn't seem to have the financial worries that I had. After talking with them, what I found out about their families and cultures would change my life forever.

For instance, both of these guys had help from family and friends in getting a head start in business and in life in general. They told me that major milestones such as graduations, weddings, and the purchase of a first home were often marked with monetary gifts. The Jewish Bar Mitzvah, for instance, was not only a coming-of-age ceremony, but a time when family and friends bestowed money upon the celebrant. Both of my colleagues had amassed more than $150,000 in their own personal investment portfolios by age twenty-five, and I had basically nothing. They told me that every time someone in their family died, like an uncle, aunt, or cousin, they usually received a sizable inheritance. I looked at these two guys in amazement and said, "Man, no wonder you all don't cry at funerals!" You see, they had wealth, and I had only income. Wealth is better.

IT'S NOT WHAT YOU MAKE;
IT'S WHAT YOU KEEP

"Income without wealth is just flash without cash," said Rev. Jesse Jackson and his son, Jesse Jackson Jr., in their book, *It's About the Money.* There's nothing behind it. It can be gone in an instant. If you work for a company, you could be fired or downsized and your salary could evaporate overnight. That's because income is *paycheck*-related, and wealth is *asset*-related. Income supplies life's necessities, like food, shelter, and clothing. Wealth, on the other hand, is a surplus that can create income.

Stories abound of prominent people who came from humble backgrounds, excelled in sports or the arts, and commanded high salaries but lost them. They were cheated by unscrupulous advisers or were simply reckless with their money. Although they were rich, they practiced the habits of the poor, and that led to their undoing.[4]

Believe it or not, many of my wealthy clients don't have incredibly high incomes. Some of them are worth $2 million, and their incomes have never been more than $150,000. Conversely, there are others I know who have made $2 million, and are only worth $100,000. That's because they spent most of the $2 million. The beautiful thing about wealth is that it is directly transferable from generation to generation, thus assuring that position, power, and opportunity can remain in your family's hands. Income can't do that.

In the African-American culture, we need to realize that making money doesn't mean anything if we consume it all. *The issue is not how much we make but how much we spend and keep.* We must learn how to turn our money into wealth. Research shows that we tend to be wage earners rather than business owners, renters rather than homeowners, and spenders rather than savers—all poor behaviors that limit our ability to attain wealth.

INCREASE YOUR NET WORTH THROUGH ASSETS

One day a couple came into my office, and they were cleaner than my grandma's chitlins. They had more than $250,000 in income, expensive designer clothes, a top-of-the-line BMW, a huge house, and all the things that said they were living large and doing well. But as they began to reveal their personal financial situation to me, I quickly found out that everything that glitters is not gold. They had a truckload of credit cards that were all maxed out. Their mortgage and car loan payments, along with their extravagant lifestyle, ate up most of their income. When I subtracted their liabilities (what they owed creditors) from their assets (what they actually owned), they were, literally, not worth a dime. They were doing what a lot of people do—pretending to be rich. The Bible tells us in Proverbs 13:7 that "there is one who pretends to be rich, but has nothing; another pretends to be poor, but has great wealth."

One of the best and most accurate indicators of our outward wealth is *net worth*. But what exactly does net worth mean? That's a foreign word to some of us in the Black community. We focus so much on what we make instead of what we are worth. Total net worth means determining the dollar value of everything you own and totaling the whole sum, then subtracting from this sum all the debts that you owe. The final number is your net worth. It is important to understand that it is not always easy to put a dollar value on the things you own. Sometimes people use the dollar value they paid for an item as the actual value but don't take into account that some things depreciate in value, such as cars. You may have paid $25,000 for the car you own, but now it may only be worth $15,000.

Sometimes people have a minus net worth, which means your liabilities are greater than your assets. If this is the case for you, please don't get discouraged. There is hope. The first time I computed my net worth, I was in my mid-twenties, and it was deep in the negative column. Now it is quite substantial. I truly believe if you follow the principles outlined in this book, your net worth will increase, too. A typical net worth statement may look something like the chart on the next page.

Net worth really gets at your financial survivability; in other words, how much wealth would you have on hand if all your debts were paid today? How long could you live comfortably without working at all?

I have found that there are usually three types of people: those who put money in assets, those who put money in liabilities, and those who put money in liabilities and think they are assets. Which one are you? The next time someone tells you he just bought a Mercedes or a Lexus because it was a "good investment," tell him that he is confused. You buy investments for them to go up, not go down. If I recommended a stock to you and told you that it would definitely go down, you wouldn't call that a good investment, would you? Of course not! Stop looking at things that depreciate in value as good investments.

According to Thomas J. Stanley, Ph.D., and William D. Danko, Ph.D., authors of the best-selling book *The Millionaire Next Door*, only

Personal Financial Statement

Date: _____

ASSETS (Present Market Value)

Cash on hand / Checking account	
Savings	
Stocks and bonds	
Cash value of life insurance	
Coins	
Home	
Other real estate	
Mortgages / Notes receivable	
Business valuation	
Automobiles	
Furniture	
Jewelry	
Other personal property	
Pension/Retirement	
Other Assets	

Total Assets:

LIABILITIES (Current amount owed)

Credit card debt	
Automobile loans	
Home mortgages	
Personal debt to relatives	
Business loans	
Educational loans	
Medical/Other past due bills	
Life insurance loans	
Bank loans	
Other debts and loans	

Total Liabilities:

NET WORTH (Total assets minus total liabilities)

3.5 percent of American households have a net worth of $1 million or more. Surprisingly, though, the average millionaire comes across as just that: average. He is not likely to drive an expensive car, live in a mansion, or wear designer labels. In fact, typical millionaires live below their means. They put their money in things that *make money*—assets like property, a business, and stocks and bonds. Unfortunately, too many of us in the African-American community put our money in things that *take money*—liabilities such as cars, clothes, and items that quickly depreciate in value. Rule number one in building generational wealth is that you must learn the difference between an asset and a liability.

THE WEALTH GAP

Every year, *Forbes* magazine lists the top income earners for the year. Many African-American celebrity entertainers and athletes are included on the highly publicized report. Names such as Bill Cosby, Michael Jackson, Oprah Winfrey, Michael Jordan, and Tiger Woods have often been included on the list. By contrast, *Forbes* has another list that documents the nation's wealthiest Americans. This particular list focuses not on income, but on wealth. It contains few, if any, African-Americans. Consider these statistics:

More than four in ten Black households (41 percent) hold less than $1,000 in net worth.[5]

Blacks have anywhere between eight dollars and nineteen dollars of wealth for every $100 that Whites possess.[6]

The median Black family's net worth is $8,300 compared with the median White family's net worth of $56,000.[7]

In the book *Black Wealth, White Wealth,* by Melvin Oliver and Thomas Shapiro, the authors make some persuasive and well-researched arguments as to why Black people's ability to accumulate wealth has been hampered throughout our history in American society. Beginning with slavery, to Jim Crow, legalized discrimination, and culminating with institutionalized racism, it has simply been more difficult for us to accumulate wealth than our White counterparts. That's because wealth is not just the assets you have now but also a legacy of the past, the authors say. I can attest to that statement, because many of my wealthy Black clients have first-generation wealth, unlike many of my White clients.

SAINTS & SINNERS

However, I believe the biggest wealth gap may not be with Black and White wealth but with Saints and Sinners. I have often wondered how many committed Christians there are on the *Forbes* lists. I don't believe there are many. If that's true, I wonder why not. Christians are always confessing and professing how rich our Father is, and how He owns cattle on a thousand hills. But for some reason, all this power is not translating into more wealth in the kingdom of God. The Bible says that the wealth of the wicked is stored up for the righteous. But just because God has laid up wealth for us doesn't mean He is going to just slap it in our hands. We've got to go get it! God feeds the birds, but He doesn't throw the worms in their mouths!

One of the saddest indictments in the Word of God, out of the mouth of God, about the people of God, is in Luke 16:8: "For the people of this world are more shrewd in dealing with their own kind than are the people of the light" (NIV).

Every time I read this verse I get a little upset, because this verse is basically saying: "When it comes to money and planning for our financial future, more often than not, sinners are smarter than saints." Why would Jesus say something like this? It's certainly not because Christians are any less intelligent than sinners, is it? Why, of course not! It's because too many of us aren't practical, we don't plan, and we aren't aggressive enough about the financial well-being of our families, the kingdom, or ourselves.

Basically, the church has messed some of us up as it relates to money. We're running around naming it and claiming it, blabbing it and grabbing it, and we're still broke! Man, I wish that was all we had to do. Everybody would be rich! It's time for men and women of God to get their financial houses in order so that we can take over! You can't have any lasting influence in this world without money. Here are a few things that I believe are hurting the wealth-building capabilities of most African-American Christians:

1. Religious escape

Too many Christians I know specialize in religious clichés and being "deep," rather than good, sound, godly stewardship. Religious activity will never make you immune from suffering the consequences of bad financial decisions. All the shouting, bucking, running around, spinning around, whooping, throwing money on the altar, and prayer lines won't get you out of debt, pay your bills, or deliver you. You still have to do something. Yes, keep on praying, and don't stop praising God for your breakthrough, but when you get finished, go to work! Take care of business! Stop using the Bible, the church, and Jesus, as a crutch— as an excuse for your laziness. Take care of your responsibilities! Pray as if it all depends on God, and work as if it all depends on you.

2. Lack of knowledge

God states in Hosea 4:6 that "my people are destroyed from lack of knowledge" (NIV). The biggest impediment I have seen in the lives of most Christians is financial ignorance. Now I don't mean that in a negative sense. There is nothing wrong with being ignorant about something —we all are—but there is everything wrong with not educating your ignorance. Everybody should know how to handle money and make wise financial decisions. Unfortunately, basic money-management skills are not taught enough in our schools, homes, or churches. Ninety-five percent of the people I have counseled who were under severe financial distress didn't have to be in their situation. Most of the time, bad decisions got them there. Their dilemma could have been avoided if they simply knew the Word of God, or if they had sought the wise counsel of someone who would tell them the truth. God's people need to educate themselves by reading the Word of God and other books, both secular and Christian, that teach about good money-management skills.

3. *Lottery mentality*

This is the get-rich-quick mentality. There are a lot of Christians who have a lottery mentality—those who try to luck their way into wealth. There are people out there who prey on church folks because they know how gullible we are. Too many of us want to get something for nothing. When I hear about certain financial schemes in the church and how I can make big money quickly, I run. I just know better. God doesn't work that way. Now some Christians play the real lottery and some play the Christian lottery. We'll talk about the real lottery in the chapter on investing (chapter 8). You are probably wondering, What's the Christian lottery? It's when you treat your church like a casino and the offering container like a slot machine. It's when your giving ceases to be worship. You are just giving to get—to hit the jackpot, to get rich quick, while all your casino buddies (church members) cheer you on. Giving is an act of worship. Don't diminish it with an act of greed.

4. *Poverty mentality*

This kind of mentality manifests itself in so many ways. I've seen people with money as well as people who don't have money that have a poverty mentality. How do you know if you have a poverty mentality? Here are just a few signs: 1) You are constantly struggling financially, and you try to justify where you are. You act as if there is some kind of virtue in being broke, as if it brings you closer to God. In essence, you are scared of money. You fear success. Even when you get money, it goes through your hands. You actually feel more comfortable struggling than living in prosperity. 2) You don't feel you deserve to live well and to have nice things. This is also a sign of low self-esteem. 3) You are critical of men and women of God who have a lot of money, especially preachers. 4) You are stingy and afraid to give according to God's Word. 5) You fear that others are always trying to take your money or rip you off. 6) You are always looking for God to do the miraculous for you. You always need something big to happen in your financial life. You view prosperity as an event, not a process.

5. Nonacceptance of the delayed gratification philosophy

The apostle Paul exhorts us in Romans 12:2 not to "be conformed to this world, but be transformed by the renewing of your mind[s]." Americans basically live in a microwave, instant-gratification society. Just about everything we desire, we can get quickly. We have computers that are increasingly faster, lightning-quick Internet access, cell phones, fancy paging, and e-mail systems. All of these things are designed to get us what we want instantly. But God is not necessarily like that. He's an "on time" God but not always a "right now" God. I see too many people get in financial trouble because they spend foolishly and presume upon God. In other words, they go out, spend, get in debt, and then expect God to bail them out. They want everything right now. Sometimes the best financial strategy you can have is to just wait. Save your money, buy things with cash, and pray about your purchases.

6. New luxury-car payments

Blacks on average are six times more likely than Whites to own a Mercedes, and the average income of a Black that buys a Jaguar is about one-third less than that of a White purchaser of the luxury vehicle. I have seen people's car payments do more to ruin their financial lives and rob them of wealth than anything else. We will talk more about this issue in the chapter on debt (chapter 4). Remember, new cars lose tremendous value in their first two to three years of use. Luxury cars always cost more to maintain, insure, and repair. If you are going to drive in style, make sure you can afford it. Also, make sure you are not sacrificing your future or the future of your kids over a car payment. What if that money was invested for your retirement or your children's or grandchildren's college education?

7. A good job

I know it sounds strange to say that a "good job" keeps people from attaining wealth, but in many cases it does. For example, having a good job usually means the following: 1) you went to college; 2) you have a nice position of which you are proud with a company; 3) you have a good image and respect from people; 4) you have good benefits and the promise of future advancement. Remember what I said earlier: Paychecks don't build wealth; assets do.

When I started in the investment profession, I found that the people who had the most money were not necessarily the engineers, executives, and corporate types. The white-collar worker gets the respect, but in many cases it's the Laundromat owner, the body shop owner, and the plumber who have the wealth.

You might have heard the story about the doctor who called the plumber to fix his water pipes. After the plumber finished the job, he handed the doctor the bill. The doctor went ballistic when he saw how much he had been charged. The doctor shouted at him, "This is highway robbery. I can't afford this!" The plumber shot back, "I couldn't either when I was a doctor!"

You need to ask yourself whether you want to be rich or whether you want to be famous. Proverbs 12:9 (AMP) says, "Better is he who is lightly esteemed but works for his own support, than he who assumes honor for himself and lacks bread." Not enough people I know own their own business, especially in the African-American community. More than 50 percent of college-educated African-Americans derive their income from the government, while less than 2 percent secure their income through business ownership. African-Americans who have their own businesses have five times the net worth of those who earn their incomes through salaries. For every one thousand members of our race, there are nine businesses, while in the larger White community there are sixty-four businesses per one thousand.

8. *Inability to understand and practice group economics*

The first seven impediments to wealth were geared more toward the individual; however, this one is geared more toward Blacks collectively. Unfortunately, 93 percent of our income is spent outside the community. The Black dollar turns over less than once on average before it leaves the Black community. Asians turn their money over nine times in their communities, and Whites turn their money over eight times before it leaves. You don't have to be a rocket scientist to see what that means. There is no way you can expect any kind of economic stability when you have that kind of cash outflow. Keeping money in a tighter circle makes the circle stronger. If more money stayed within the African-American community, there would be less unemployment and more revenues for businesses. This is a win-win situation for everybody. Failure to practice group economics further impoverishes Black communities. We dis-empower ourselves when we fail to spend some of our hard earned money with each other. Unfortunately, while most ethnic groups realize that there is strength in numbers, many Blacks do not necessarily see strength in grouping themselves with other Blacks. Too many of us think that it's un-Christian, or too "militant" to think this way. That's because we've been conditioned not to trust one another and help one another. Dr. Martin Luther King Jr. said, "Whenever Pharaoh wanted to keep the slaves in slavery, he kept them fighting among themselves." We must reverse years of self-deprecating thinking about one another in order to control our resources and mantain a strong sense of community. Institutional power is always more potent and long-lasting than individual power.

THE POWER TO MAKE WEALTH

When it comes to money, Deuteronomy 8:18 is one of the most popular and frequently quoted verses in the Bible. What I usually hear from people sounds something like this: "You know, Brother Lee, the Bible says God gives us the power to make wealth," and then they close their Bibles, shout, and dance. They act as if that's the end of the verse.

Now what they have quoted is not wrong; it's just not complete. Indeed, God does give us the power to make wealth, and that's enough to shout about, but the rest of the verse tells us why He gives us that power: "But you shall remember the Lord your God, for it is He who is giving you power to make wealth, that He may confirm His covenant which He swore to your fathers, as it is this day."

The reason God gives us the power to make wealth is the covenant. Well, what's the covenant? That's found in Genesis 12:2–3: "And I will make you a great nation, and I will bless you, and make your name great; and so you shall be a blessing; and I will bless those who bless you, and the one who curses you I will curse. And in you all the families of the earth shall be blessed."

This covenant was made with Abraham. As a Christian, our spiritual family line, humanly speaking, begins with Father Abraham. We are all spiritual descendants of him. Therefore, what God is saying to Abraham applies to every believer. In essence, what God is saying is, "I am going to bless you, and make your name great, so that you can be a blessing." You see the reason God wants to get wealth *to* us is so He can get wealth *through* us. God has a purpose for everything He gives us, and that includes money. Below I have listed the five primary purposes for wealth.

1. To bless you

God wants to bless you and give you the desires of your heart. The Bible says that He actually delights in our prosperity and in meeting our needs. There are many godly people in the Bible that were blessed with great material abundance. Some of them were just flat-out living large! Abraham was rich, Solomon was superrich, and Job was pretty well off, too. Don't ever think that God doesn't want you to prosper, because He does. I believe that John's letter to Gaius in 3 John 1:2 summarizes what God desires for us: "Beloved, I pray that in all respects you may prosper and be in good health, just as your soul prospers."

2. To take care of your family

God cares deeply about the financial well-being of your family. In fact, He cares so much that 1 Timothy 5:8 says, "If anyone does not provide for his own, and especially for those of his household, he has denied the faith and is worse than an unbeliever." God wants your family to be blessed through you.

3. To give to the kingdom

One of the main reasons God gives you wealth is so that you can sow it back into the kingdom. As a matter of fact, 2 Corinthians 9:10 tells us that God will multiply our seed for sowing as we continue to give to Him. Don't take your giving lightly. Commit at least 10 percent of your gross income to the Lord's work.

4. To carry out your calling

God blesses all of us in different measures for different reasons. In the parable of the talents, the master gave each servant a different amount of money, each according to his own ability. That's why it doesn't make sense to compare what you have with somebody else or to try to keep up with the Joneses. You have to consider what God's plan is for your life. God blesses some people with lots of money, a big house, and a nice car simply because their calling requires it—not because they are any better than you, or because God favors them more than He does you.

5. To help others

There is nothing like being a blessing to somebody else. We are blessed to be a blessing. As the Lord prospers you, always be on the lookout for someone who may be in need. Don't just think about yourself and your family all the time.

My wife and I would ask the Lord to show us families who needed financial help at our church. Sometimes, without our knowing any details, God would drop a person on our hearts, and we would go and give them money. Man, you should have seen their faces light up. Little did we know that some of these people had been praying for a financial miracle. Sometimes people's lights were about to be cut off or their car repossessed. God used us because we were looking to be a blessing to someone else.

THE DANGERS OF OUTWARD WEALTH

Deuteronomy 8:18 begins with the phrase "But you shall remember the Lord your God." The word *remember* is there for a reason. Unfortunately, after God blesses some folks, they don't remember who blessed them. They simply forget God. Scripture identifies a number of dangers associated with wealth and material possessions in Deuteronomy 31:20: "For when I bring them into the land flowing with milk and honey, which I swore to their fathers, and they have eaten and are satisfied and became prosperous, then they will turn to other gods and serve them, and spurn Me and break My covenant."

Someone once observed, "For every ninety-nine people who can be poor and remain close to the Lord, only one can become wealthy and still maintain close fellowship with Him." A lot of people can pass the test of poverty, but not many pass the test of prosperity. When we are broke, busted, and disgusted, we don't have any choice but to hold on to God. But once we become wealthy and more self-sufficient, we often take the Lord for granted because we no longer think we have as much need of Him. Don't let that happen to you. Don't let riches create pride in your life or compete with God. Enjoy the blessings that the Lord bestows upon you, but keep Him first.

Chapter Two

WHAT'S GOD GOT
TO DO WITH IT?

*K*eenan and Jackie were desperately seeking answers to their financial woes. When Jackie called me on the telephone, I could tell by her voice that something was wrong. In a very serious tone, she said, "Lee . . . me and Keenan need to come talk to you and your wife tonight. Is that possible?" I said, "Tonight? What's going on? Is everything all right?" She took a deep breath, then in an exasperated tone said, "No, things aren't all right. Keenan is really tripping again about the money." I could hear Keenan in the background hollering, "Hey, brother, she's the one tripping!" I sensed that things were getting pretty heated, so we set the appointment for seven o' clock that evening.

When they got to our house they were fairly cordial, but I could tell that whatever was bothering them was as serious as a heart attack. Keenan and Jackie were both committed Christians and had been married about two and a half years. They had a one-year-old son. Both had attended the same college, where they met, but only Jackie graduated. They both had decent-paying jobs, Keenan as an insurance salesman, and Jackie as a nurse. Jackie was on salary, and Keenan earned his money on commissions. Since they had been married, Jackie had always earned more money than her husband.

Jackie started venting first. She told us that they presently had all their money in joint checking and savings accounts. Recently, however, Jackie had made the decision to have her own accounts separate from Keenan's. She said his propensity for writing checks that bounced and not keeping good records had gotten the couple into some financial trouble. Furthermore, she said that she made more money than Keenan and that her income was basically supporting the family. Keenan's commissions were sporadic at best, she said, and she couldn't depend on him financially.

Jackie decided she was going to take control of her life and her money by opening her own account to which Keenan would not have access. That did not sit too well with Keenan, who saw Jackie's move as an attempt to undermine his authority. He stated that if she was going to separate the money, then maybe the accounts ought not to be the only thing to separate. It was his opinion that no money should be kept from him and that all funds should be under his purview as the "head of the house." Jackie felt that all the money should be turned over to her because she was a better manager.

While a family crisis such as Keenan and Jackie's may be foreign to some of us, the message is clear: The issue of money in the life of a Christian is just as important as any issue we face. Statistics say that 50 percent of marriages end in divorce, and 80 percent of those fail due to finance-related issues. No wonder some people say that the most sensitive nerve in the body is the one that leads to the wallet! The matter concluded with their keeping their money in joint accounts. More important, Jackie realized that even though she was the primary breadwinner, it didn't give her the right to disrespect Keenan as the leader of their home. Keenan, on the other hand, needed to let go of his pride and give up some control of their money. I'm happy to say that, over time, Keenan and Jackie did resolve their conflict. There are no more power struggles and heated arguments over money, because they finally gained the Lord's perspective on their finances.

TO WHOM MUCH IS GIVEN,
MUCH IS REQUIRED

Today, Blacks control more than $500 billion of annual income. That would rank the African-American community economically among the fifteenth wealthiest nations in the world. However, our prosperity has grown faster than our understanding of personal financial stewardship. The issue today is not how much we have, but what we do with what we have.

For four hundred years, our ancestors here had little or no access to capital. Instead, they themselves were traded as a form of currency. Slaves were by law not able to own property or accumulate assets. For centuries, many Blacks had no practice in stewarding private property. Perhaps that explains why sometimes when we get our hands on money, we do go "mad," as George Washington Carver put it back in 1931, "spending it as if there isn't going to be a tomorrow."

In contrast, no matter how poor Whites were, they had the right—if they were males, that is—and the ability, to buy land, enter contracts, own businesses, and develop wealth assets that could build equity and economic self-sufficiency for themselves and their families. Some argue that it was our inability to participate in and develop a habit of savings during slavery that directly accounts for the low wealth development and bad stewardship habits among Blacks today.[1]

Authors Melvin Oliver and Thomas Shapiro, in their book *Black Wealth, White Wealth*, stated that although many slaves were not able to amass wealth, they did, in large numbers, acquire assets through thrift, intelligence, industry, and their owner's liberal paternalism. These assets were used to buy their own and their loved ones' freedom, however, and thus did not form the core of a material legacy that could be passed from generation to generation. Whites could use their wealth for the future; Black slaves' savings could only buy the freedom that Whites took for granted.

But times are different now. As Susan Taylor, former editor of *Essence* magazine, wrote, "We are the first generation of Black people in four hundred years who can live out our dreams." Unfortunately, far too many of us have had our dreams turn into nightmares. Many of us who love the Lord haven't learned yet how to be good stewards of our resources. This is primarily the job of the family and the church, and we have failed miserably at it.

Like Keenan and Jackie, there are too many people who completely separate God and His Word from all financial aspects of their lives, and perhaps just as many who overspiritualize the part God plays in their finances. However, how we should handle our money is clearly revealed in Scripture. Simply put: God has a part to play, and we have a part. Much of the frustration people experience in handling money is because they have some wrong ideas about this division of responsibilities— which is our part and which is God's part.

A STEWARD'S RESPONSIBILITY

Our part is best described as that of a steward. The Greek word for "steward" is *oikonomos*, which can be translated into the English words *manager* or *supervisor*. In Scripture, the position of steward is one of great responsibility. He or she is one who is entrusted with another's wealth or property and charged with the responsibility of managing it for the benefit of the owner.

What I do every day as an investment adviser can be compared to a steward. I oversee and manage investment portfolios for my clients, and my goal is to choose investments that will increase in value. The person who takes care of passengers on a cruise ship is called a steward. The people who oversee an airline flight used to be called stewardesses. They don't own the plane, but they are responsible for carrying out the captain's orders. They manage the flight on behalf of the owner, the airline, so the flight is safe and orderly.

Even though we are all stewards, most people reason that the money they have earned belongs to them, and they have a right to do with it whatever they please. However, the biblical view of handling money is radically different. Stewardship, by its very nature, involves two concepts: ownership and accountability.

Christian stewardship begins with the understanding that all we have belongs to God, that He has made us stewards, or managers, of His possessions and that the Lord will reward us according to the actions and the attitude of our stewardship.

"It is required in stewards," the apostle Paul wrote, "that a man be found faithful" (1 Corinthians 4:2 KJV). Before we can be faithful, however, we have to know what we are required to do with that which has been entrusted to us.

DO BUSINESS WITH THIS

In Luke 19:11–27, Jesus told a powerful parable about the kingdom of God and how we should handle His possessions. This powerful passage lays out the standards of our responsibilities as stewards and how our stewardship will be evaluated. Let's unfold this important passage. "While they were listening to these things, Jesus went on to tell a parable, because He was near Jerusalem, and they supposed that the kingdom of God was going to appear immediately. So He said, 'A nobleman went to a distant country to receive a kingdom for himself, and then return. And he called ten of his slaves, and gave them ten minas and said to them, "Do business with this until I come back"'" (vv. 11–13).

Now it's obvious in the parable that Christ is the nobleman going away to lay claim to the kingdom. The "distant country" is heaven, from which He will return one day to establish His visible kingdom.

But in the meantime, the King gives us gifts and responsibilities to look after until He returns. He longs for us to be faithful and diligent in doing our duty, and He is going to reward those who are faithful and severely judge those who do nothing.

There are seven distinct elements of faithful stewardship that are found in this parable.

1. Prosperity is a process, not an event.

The first thing we must understand about this parable is why Jesus told it. Luke 19:11 says that Jesus told the parable because "He was near Jerusalem, and they supposed that the kingdom of God was going to appear immediately." The disciples and the people with Jesus were eagerly anticipating an immediate deliverance, and Jesus was basically telling them that there would be a delay, and here's what He needed them to do in the meantime.

Financially speaking, I'm concerned that many Christians today are like those to whom Jesus was talking. Far too many of us are expecting an immediate deliverance from our financial problems (an event) instead of learning how to practice good stewardship on a day-to-day basis (a process). Many of us think that all we have to do is press a button, like the one on a microwave oven, and then presto . . . instant prosperity! We are pulling levers, standing in prosperity lines, getting hands laid on us, repeating catchy phrases, and basically asking God to do something that is against His nature.

As a parent, I know that I am not going to give my seven year old the keys to my car and tell him to drive it. That would be stupid on my part and would put my son in great danger. Likewise, God is not going to put wealth into your hands until you have demonstrated the character, maturity, and stewardship skills required to handle it. God doesn't want to put your life in danger by giving you more than you can handle. If some us had what we prayed for, it would simply ruin us. Read the parable of the prodigal son in Luke 15:11–32. It perfectly illustrates what can happen to a person who's not prepared to handle what's been given to him.

Brothers and sisters, stop trying to microwave the things of God. You can't microwave wealth, character, wisdom, and maturity. You can't microwave your debt away either. For some of you, it took ten years for you to get into the financial mess that you're in, and you're not going to necessarily get out of your mess in six months. If God wanted to, He could deliver you instantly, but He's after something deeper in you. God cares more about your *character* than your *cash*.

2. *God owns it all, and we are managers of His assets.*

The nobleman in Luke 19 gave the slaves a portion of money that belonged to him. The slaves didn't contribute anything; the money belonged to the nobleman. Likewise, everything we have belongs to God. God created it all, so it's all God's property.

Now this principle may be easy to state, but living it out is another story. The fact is, God's ownership is inescapable. The Bible clearly states that God is the sole owner of everything. "The earth is the Lord's, and all it contains" (Psalm 24:1). Scripture even reveals specific items God owns. Leviticus 25:23 identifies Him as owner of all the land: "The land . . . shall not be sold permanently, for the land is Mine." Haggai 2:8 reveals that "the silver is Mine and the gold is Mine." And in Psalm 50:10, the Lord tells us, "For every beast of the forest is Mine, the cattle on a thousand hills."

The Lord is the creator of all things, and He has never transferred the ownership of His creation to people. The money that you have in your pocket right now was printed on paper that was ground from the pulp of trees that grew on God's property. The car that you drive was shaped out of metal whose elements were dug from God's earth. The clothes on your back are only there because God made them possible.[2]

Since God owns it all, and everything we have belongs to Him, then whatever we do with what God gives us has a spiritual dimension to it. In other words, *every spending decision becomes a spiritual decision.* No longer do we have the attitude, "Lord, what do You want me to do with my money?" It becomes, "Lord, what do You want me to do with Your money?" When we have this attitude and prayerfully handle His money according to God's wishes, spending and saving decisions become as spiritual as giving decisions.

The beautiful thing about having someone else own something is that when it breaks, the owner has to fix it. It's just like renting an apartment. The landlord is ultimately responsible to fix things that break in the renter's living quarters. The same is true with our finances and our life. When you let the Lord own you and your money, when the money runs out, He has to supply it. And since God owns it all anyway, you know that God can provide all of your financial needs regardless of the situation.

3. Your practicality determines your spirituality.

The nobleman's command to his slaves "Do business with this until I come back" (Luke 19:13) gets to the heart of the steward's responsibility.

The Greek word for "business" is the word for which we get the English word *pragmatic*. *Pragmatic* means to be practical. Therefore, the command here is for the slaves to do something practical. And there is nothing more practical than being a good financial steward. The problem with a lot of Christians is that we think the more spiritual we are, the less pragmatic we should be. Actually, the opposite is true. Spiritual people are people who have their practical lives in order.

I remember a story about a man who died in a flood while waiting on God to save him. The man was already surrounded by floodwaters when two men in a Jeep drove by and offered to drive him to safety. The man refused their offer, saying, "I'm just going to trust God to save me."

Later, as the water was still rising, a man in a rowboat floated by the man's house and tried to convince him to get in the boat so he could be taken to dry land. Again, the man refused, saying, "I'm just going to trust God to save me."

When the rising tide forced the man to the rooftop, a helicopter flew by and dropped a ladder for him to climb aboard. He waved the helicopter off, shouting once again, "I'm just going to trust God to save me."

Shortly after that, the man was drowned by the floodwaters. Angrily he stood before Saint Peter at the pearly gates and shouted, "I'm pretty angry at God because I trusted Him, and He let me drown." To which Saint Peter replied, "God's pretty angry at you too. He sent the Jeep, the boat, and the helicopter to save you, but you were too stubborn to get in any of them!"

Seriously, don't be so religious that you ignore the practical things you need to do as a steward. Remember this: *Just because God can do anything doesn't mean He's going to do everything.* You do the possible and let God do the impossible.

In Luke 16:11 we read, "Therefore if you have not been faithful in the use of unrighteous mammon, who will entrust the true riches to you?" In this verse Jesus equates how we handle money (which is a very practical thing) with the quality of our spiritual life. If we handle our money properly according to the principles of Scripture, our fellowship with Christ will grow stronger. However, if we manage money unfaithfully, our fellowship with Him will suffer.

4. Money is a tool.

In Luke 19:13 the nobleman commands, "Do business" (NASB), "Put this money to work" (NIV), and "Occupy" (KJV). The Greek word for "occupy" is *pragmateuomai*, which means to get busy, to do business, to work for gain, to trade for profit. As stewards, God gives us money as a *tool* to use, to advance the kingdom of God. The servant of God is to labor diligently, using all that the Lord has given him to look after.

Now don't forget that this is still a command to do something practical with your money. This is not a command to do something spiritual per se, like giving. We will talk about the importance of tithes and offerings in chapter 7. The kind of business the text is referring to are things such as investing, saving, trading, being outstanding in your field of expertise, etc. We need billions of dollars for the work of the kingdom, and it's time for the saints of God to get serious about money management and business in general.

5. Money is a test.

Again in Luke 19:15, we are told that the nobleman did return, and the day of accounting did arrive. Every servant was called to report on what he had done with the money that was given to him.

The purpose of giving the servants the minas was really not about making money. The purpose was to *test* them, to show how capable and responsible they were. It was a time of trial. Could they be trusted with responsibility? The leaders who are needed to rule in God's kingdom must be strong and responsible. The nobleman's purpose, just like Christ's, is to develop distinguished leaders that are decisive, firm, and strong.

Here are several tests that we all have to pass in order to qualify for the kind of financial blessings the Lord wants to bestow upon us.

A Test of All that You Have

We are charged to be faithful in handling 100 percent of our money, not just 10 percent. Unfortunately, many churches have concentrated only on teaching people how to handle 10 percent of our income— the area of giving. Although this is crucial, we have allowed Christians to learn how to handle the other 90 percent from the world's perspective, not from the Lord's perspective. Tithing doesn't excuse you from faithfully managing the rest of your money. As a matter of fact, I know plenty of folks who tithe, and they still have severe financial problems. Bad financial habits like overspending, impulse spending, and credit-card abuse with the 90 percent will nullify the blessings of the tithe.

A Test of How You Handle Small Things

I meet a lot of people who say, "Brother Lee, if I had a million dollars I would tithe, or I would do this, and I would do that." I always tell them that what you do with the money you have right now is what you would do if you had more. If you are a bad steward with a $15,000 income, you'll be a bad steward with $150,000, unless you change your habits.

Being poor, broke, on welfare, or rich doesn't excuse you from being faithful with what you have. God doesn't care what you would do with a million dollars; He's concerned about what you're doing with the ten, fifty, and one hundred dollars you've got right now.

Luke 16:10 reads, "He who is faithful in a very little thing is faithful also in much; and he who is unrighteous in a very little thing is unrighteous also in much." How you handle the little either qualifies or disqualifies you for much. The little actually determines how you will handle much. How do you know if your child is going to take care of his first car? Observe how he cared for his bicycle. If we have the character to be faithful with small things, the Lord knows He can trust us with greater responsibilities. If you're not tithing from your $40,000 income, you are going to have a hard time tithing your $200,000 income. "Small things are small things," Hudson Taylor, the great missionary statesman, said, "but faithfulness with a small thing is a big thing."

A Test of Other People's Things

Faithfulness with another's possessions will, in some measure, determine the amount with which you are entrusted. "And if you have not been faithful in the use of that which is another's, who will give you that which is your own?" (Luke 16:12). This is a principle that is often overlooked.

Once I loaned a guy our minivan for about a month. I was a little apprehensive about how it would be returned, but when he brought it back, it literally looked like a new vehicle. It had been shampooed, vacuumed, and even detailed. I hardly recognized my own vehicle! I'll tell you, if that guy ever needs to borrow something from me again, I probably wouldn't hesitate to help him.

Are you faithful with another's possessions? When someone allows you to use something, are you careful to return it in good shape? I am certain some people have not been given more because they have been unfaithful with the possessions of others.

A Test of Your Character

Depending upon how it is handled, money proves a blessing or a curse to its possessor. Either the person becomes master of the money, or the money becomes master of the person.

During my one year of professional football with the New York Giants, I saw quite a few guys change for the worse after they signed their big-league contracts. After some of them started to earn their six- or seven-figure salaries, they began to live out some of their wildest fantasies. Some were unfaithful to their wives and spent lavishly on cars, clothes, jewelry, and on their mistresses. Surveys confirm a strong moral decline in people who are used to having what they want materially:

Among both men and women the incidence of marital infidelity rises in conjunction with an increase in income. Of the married men earning

$20,000 a year, only 31 percent conduct extracurricular love affairs; of the men earning more than $60,000, 70 percent.[3]

Now did the money change these people? Did the money cause their adultery? Or did the money magnify what was already in their hearts? I believe it was the latter. Throughout Scripture we find an intimate correlation between the development of a person's character and how he or she handles money.

6. Money is a testimony.

In Luke 19 again, the nobleman has returned from his journey, and he's ready to call his servants to account for how they used their minas.

The first servant came and said, "Master, your mina has made ten minas more." The master said to him, "Well done, good slave, because you have been faithful in a very little thing, you are to be in authority over ten cities" (vv. 16–17). And the second came saying, "Your mina, master, has made five minas." And he said to him also, "You are to be over five cities" (vv. 18–19). Then there's the third slave. He brought his mina and said, "Master, here is your mina, which I kept put away in a handkerchief; for I was afraid of you, because you are an exacting man" (vv. 20–21).

The three results illustrate the three courses of action taken by God's servants: being very faithful, faithful, and unfaithful. The two faithful servants were rewarded, but one was 1,000 percent faithful, the other 500 percent faithful. The master commended the servant who labored 1,000 percent, "Well done." There will be nothing like hearing Jesus say, "Well done!" when you show up at His judgment seat. The servant who served 500 percent was not personally commended. The servant who did not work at all received nothing. As a matter of fact, he even tried to justify his behavior by making up excuses. This very excuse, along with his unfaithfulness, resulted in his being called "wicked" (NIV). Now, he was not being called wicked for what he did but for what he didn't do. His sin was the sin of omission, not the sin of commission. He didn't do anything because he felt the master required too much and was too strict.

I don't know about you, but I want my testimony to be "well done," instead of "you wicked servant." When you handle God's resources in a way that pleases Him, He wants to show you off.

7. If you don't use it, you lose it.

The servant who had the best return was given the reward of the servant who did nothing. Why? Very simply, because he had proven that he could handle any amount of responsibility. He had taken a little (one pound) and used it to the maximum. The better you manage your money, the more money comes your way.

As a steward, you must remember that *God expects increase on what He loans to us.* Stewardship isn't just about management, it's about increase. Now you know why some of the rich get richer and some of the poor get poorer. If a man does not use his gift, he will lose it to someone who will use it better. That may seem kind of cold, but that's the way God thinks. Just as a man with an arm would lose his arm if he didn't use it, so will we lose our wealth and our good testimony if we are not faithful stewards.

REAL SOLUTIONS

As we apply the principles of God's economy to our everyday lives, we will begin to get out of debt, spend more wisely, start saving for our future goals, and give more money to the work of Christ.

What's God got to do with it? He has everything to do with it. The Bible offers real solutions to today's financial problems. Each of the following chapters deals with one of the specific areas necessary to equip us to become faithful stewards.

Chapter Three

———— ❧ ❧ ————

CHARTING YOUR FINANCIAL DESTINY

*I*n the very first financial class I held at my church, a young lady named Lynn sat in the front row. Life had been hard for Lynn, who, like her mother, had been a teenage mother. Lynn gave birth to three children before her seventeenth birthday, lived on welfare, and never finished high school. She was married at twenty-four, but the terrible financial struggles continued for her and her family. They were always late on their bills and consequently were always having to move—twelve times in seven years to be exact. During that same period, they went through fifteen very used cars. The financial pressures, as well as the verbal and physical abuse from her husband, began to take their toll. Though Lynn did not want the marriage to end, finally she and her husband divorced. His departure was emotionally devastating for her.

After the first class, Lynn approached me and told me that the class was her last resort. After speaking with her about her problems, it seemed at first that her situation was so bad that it would be impossible to get out. She was deeply in debt, had a low-paying job, three children to support, and no plans for her future. Like a lot of people, she was like a ship without a rudder, wandering aimlessly in the waters of life, being tossed back and forth by her circumstances. I recommended to Lynn that we start planning her life by setting goals and then working toward achieving those goals. I was able to get Lynn out of a survival mentality and into a planning and doing mentality. For the first time in her life, Lynn was determined to change her circumstances. What happened in the next nine months was nothing short of phenomenal.

Lynn got a new job with a cellular telephone company as a customer-service representative. After six months, she was asked to fill in as an acting supervisor. Three months after that, she was hired for the supervisor position with a pay increase that more than doubled her income. Lynn, having only a GED, was making more money than she thought possible. Lynn is now debt-free. She lives on a budget, tithes, and saves her money. She has even bought a three-bedroom home and is taking classes working toward a bachelor's degree in business management. Lynn's life improved drastically because she found the courage to plan her work and then work her plan. You can do that, too.

YOU NEED TO JOIN THIS FIVE PERCENT

Many years ago, master motivator Napoleon Hill explained the "top 5 percent" theory in his book *Think and Grow Rich*:

"If you approach one hundred men and women of equal education, equal skills, and equal background at age twenty-five and ask if they would like to be wealthy in the field of their choice, you'll notice a sparkle in their eyes, an eagerness toward life, and a keenness in their manner—for they truly wish to be rich."

Now project these same individuals forty years into the future—allowing for time, growth, experience, and opportunity. At the end of those forty years, with the chance to be great in the field of their choice, in the richest nation on the face of the earth—only one will be rich! Four will be financially independent, thirty will be dead, and sixty-five will be forced to rely on any number of government programs in order to survive the remaining years of their lives.

Think for a moment of those whom you pass on the street, no matter how large or small the city, no matter its location, and regardless of the race or creed of its inhabitants—only five out of one hundred people will achieve their financial goals. Only 5 percent!

And what of the other 95 percent? Unfortunately, they just drift along, hoping and wishing that someday their "change" would come. They are waiting on the lottery to hit or the long-lost millionaire uncle to die and leave them money. These are able-bodied men and women who've allowed the winds of circumstance to blow them in any direction.

Why, in this land of plenty, is there such a disheartening ending to so many lives? What happened to the sparkle in their eyes and their eagerness toward life? What became of their hopes, their dreams, and their plans?

GOD IS THE ULTIMATE PLANNER

In Jeremiah 29:11 the Lord says, "'For I know the plans I have for you,' declares the Lord, 'plans for welfare and not for calamity to give you a future and a hope.'" This passage clearly states that the Lord has a plan for our future—not just any plan either, but a great one! Now if God, who is all-knowing, operates by a plan, then doesn't it seem logical that we, as mere human beings, should also incorporate planning and goal-setting into our lives? Everything the Lord does, He has a plan for. Our Lord does nothing haphazardly. He had a plan to redeem us from the penalty of sin; that plan was Calvary (John 3:16–17). He gave Noah a plan to build the ark (Genesis 6:14–21). He gave Joshua a plan to get into Jericho (Joshua 6:1–20). He gave Moses a plan to face Pharaoh (Exodus 3:7–10). He gave Elijah a plan when the brook dried up (1 Kings 17:2–16). God is the ultimate strategic planner.

GOD EXPECTS YOU TO MAKE PLANS

Sometimes when I speak to audiences about money management, I ask them the following questions: "By a show of hands, how many of you want to be rich?" There are always numerous hands that go up. Then I ask them, "How many of you are saving 5 to 10 percent of your income? How many of you are taking full advantage of your employer's 401(k) or other company-sponsored plan?" A lot of hands go down. Then I ask, "Who owns a least two mutual funds? How many of you are invested in the stock market?" By this time, there are not a whole lot of hands left up, especially if I'm speaking at a church. Then I say, "For those of you who put your hands down, when are you going to stop wishing for wealth and start building and planning toward it?"

In Luke 16:1–9, Jesus tells a parable about an unrighteous steward who really messed up. This parable happens to be one of the most intriguing and misunderstood passages in the entire Bible, but it perfectly underscores the importance of planning.

> The story is about "a rich man who had a manager. He got reports that the manager had been taking advantage of his position by [wasting his goods and] running up huge personal expenses. So he called him in and said, 'What's this I hear about you? You're fired. And I want a complete audit of your books.'
>
> "The manager said to himself, 'What am I going to do? I've lost my job as manager. I'm not strong enough for a laboring job, and I'm too proud to beg. . . . Ah, I've got a plan. Here's what I'll do . . . then when I'm turned out into the street [unemployed], people will take me into their houses [and give me a job].'
>
> "Then he went at it. One after another, he called in the people who were in debt to his master. He said to the first, 'How much do you owe my master?'
>
> "He replied, 'A hundred jugs of olive oil.'
>
> "The manager said, 'Here, take your bill, sit down here—quick now—write "fifty."'
>
> "To the next he said, 'And you, what do you owe?'
>
> "He answered, 'A hundred sacks of wheat.'
>
> "He said, 'Take your bill, write in "eighty."'
>
> "Now here's a surprise: The master praised the crooked manager! And why? Because he knew how to look after himself. Streetwise people

[unbelievers] are smarter in this regard than law-abiding citizens [believers]. They are on constant alert, looking for angles, surviving by their wits. I want you to be smart in the same way—but for what is *right*—using every adversity to stimulate your creative survival, to concentrate your attention on the bare essentials, so you'll live, really live, and not complacently just get by on good behavior."[1]

Now Jesus used this parable not to commend the manager for his cunning deceit. What the manager did was blatantly wrong. These people legitimately owed his master money, and he sliced their bills by 20 to 50 percent. Jesus was commending him for his concern about the future and the dedication and energy he put into planning. The unrighteous manager was sold out to pursuing a goal, and that part of his life was commendable.

So let me ask you a couple of questions. Do you have a life plan? Do you set goals for yourself? Do you put your goals on paper? Do you have a clear road map to reach your destination, or are you just winging it? Many of us spend more time planning our once-a-year vacation than we do planning our everyday financial affairs. Spiritual people have a tendency to believe that if they have faith, or if they just trust God, they don't have to plan. Many of you have been praying for a financial miracle, and God is answering your prayer by giving you a plan. It takes faith to plan. When God asked Noah to build the ark, no one had ever seen rain before, not even Noah. Noah was probably ridiculed and laughed at for building the ark, but he followed God's plan, and he and his family were saved from the Flood. Your deliverance is in the plan. Remember, if you fail to plan, then you are planning to fail.

THE DIFFERENCE
BETWEEN A GOAL AND A DREAM

Every dream needs a blueprint. I have read many definitions regarding the difference between a goal and a dream, and this is the one I like the most: A dream is what you would like to happen, but a goal is what you intend to make happen.

Financial Goals

Date: _____

GIVING GOALS:

Would like to give _____ percent of my income.

Other giving goals: _____

_____

DEBT REPAYMENT GOALS:

Would like to pay off the following debts first:

Creditor   Amount

_____   _____

_____   _____

_____   _____

_____   _____

EDUCATIONAL GOALS:

Would like to fund the following education:

Person	School	Annual Cost	Total Cost
_____	_____	_____	_____
_____	_____	_____	_____
_____	_____	_____	_____
_____	_____	_____	_____

Other educational goals: _____

_____

LIFESTYLE GOALS:

Would like to make the following major purchases (home, automobile, travel, etc.):

Item   Amount

_____   _____

_____   _____

_____   _____

_____   _____

Would like to achieve the following annual income: _____

SAVINGS AND INVESTMENT GOALS:

Would like to save _____ percent on my income.

Other savings goals: _____

_____

Would like to make the following investments: Investment

_____   _____

_____   _____

_____   _____

_____   _____

Would like to provide my/our heirs with the following: _____
_____

STARTING A BUSINESS:

Would like to invest in or begin my/our own business: _____
_____
_____

Goals For This Year

I believe the Lord wants me/us to achieve the following goals this year:

Priority	Financial Goals	Our Part	God's Part
1			
2			
3			
4			
5			

I heard another man say that a goal is a dream with a deadline. Many people dream of an ideal life that they would like to have someday, but they never really intend to pursue their dream and turn it into a reality. Goals are intentional. Goals make the dream come true.

The Bible says that faith without works is dead. What percentage of adult Americans do you think have written, specific, long-range goals? Several years ago, a national insurance company did a survey and concluded that only 3 percent had written, specific, long-range goals. Let me ask you another question. What percentage of American people at age sixty-five can put their hands on $10,000 in cash? The answer is 5 percent! Why do I ask these two questions? Because I believe they are related. Without setting specific goals, most people in this country will not achieve financial security.

If you ask most people what their goals or plans are in life, most answers will be very vague and unrealistic. They may say "happiness," or "doing God's will," or "being financially free." These are not goals; they're simply dreams and wishes desired by everyone. When I speak of goals, I mean what is it that you would like to have or be? When would you like for this to happen? A dream may be you wanting to start your own business one day. Your goal, on the other hand, will answer the question: What kind of business do you want to start? When do you want to begin your own business? A few years ago, I had a dream of spending more time with my family. My ministry commitments and busy civic and business schedule kept me away from my family too much. The dream didn't turn into a goal until I promised my wife and kids that I would be home from the office no later than six o'clock every day.

As an investment adviser, many of my clients come to me with their dreams every day. They say things like, "I want to retire at age sixty," or, "I want to make sure that if I live to age ninety, I won't run out of money," or, "I want to retire in twenty years." After I assess how much money they will need in order to reach their goal, and what the cost of living will be when they retire, I then have to get them to do what it takes to make their dream come true. That may mean setting aside extra money each month or cutting back on their spending so they will have more money to put toward their investments. Sometimes it's a sacrifice.

Are you willing to sacrifice to make your dreams come true? Will you forgo the pleasures of today so you can enjoy life the way you want to ten, twenty, or thirty years down the line? As long as what you want to do is consistent with Scripture, remember that, with God, all things are possible.

FOUR REASONS FOR SETTING GOALS

1. Goals provide guidance and direction.

Proverbs 29:18 (KJV) reads: "Where there is no vision, the people perish." Although the NIV translation is somewhat different, the impact is equally powerful: "Where there is no revelation, the people cast off restraint." What is vision? I heard one pastor say that vision is what God lets you see on "credit." Another speaker said vision is your "shall be," not your current realities. I like this definition: Vision is your "preview of coming attractions." When you are at the movies and you see previews of the movies coming out, you get excited about seeing them— that's vision.

The point is clear: Unless you have a clear understanding of where you are going, and a good mental picture of it, the probability of your getting there is limited. Sprinters on a track team know where they are going. They don't wander off the track, because they are focused on the finish line. Airplanes and ships also have a destination. When you set goals, your choices for activity become more purposeful.

I remember when my wife and I were renting an apartment and we decided that it was time to start looking for a house. We began trying to save for a down payment but had a difficult time disciplining ourselves. One year had gone by, and we hadn't saved much. Then one day we found a neighborhood that we loved. All of a sudden we got motivated, because we now had a vision of how and where we wanted to live.

We began to cut back on our spending. We brought our lunches to work instead of eating out. We put a freeze on all clothes-related spending. My wife cooked at home instead of our eating out. In just four months, we saved enough money for the down payment on our first home. It's interesting that what we tried to do in a year with no vision got done in four months with vision. We all need vision in order to stay disciplined and focused.

2. *Goals make you think strategically.*

Thinking strategically is not just for businesspeople. We all need to be strategic thinkers when it comes to our finances. Strategic thinking means to look ahead, plan ahead, and act quickly on your plans.

In Luke 16:3, the unrighteous steward asked himself the question, "What shall I do?" He knew that he was going to lose his job, so he had to think of a plan. And, boy, what a great strategic plan it was! He decided to slash the debts of the people who owed his master money. He slashed one bill by 50 percent and the other by 20 percent. Now this would be like a waitress coming to your table at a restaurant and telling you to only pay half of the bill you owed instead of the entire amount. The problem with a waitress doing this is that she doesn't have that kind of authority; only the manager or the owner of the restaurant does. So not only did the unrighteous steward mess up his master's money, but he also acted unethically toward his master's debtors. But there was a method to the steward's madness. He knew that his actions would find favor with the debtors, and they might consider hiring him after he was fired, since he did them such a big favor by discounting their bills. In other words, his strategy was to find a J-O-B! The brother knew what he wanted. He looked ahead, he planned ahead, and he acted quickly.

What do you want in life? Maybe it's a comfortable retirement, a home on the beach or in the mountains, or more time and resources to devote to the kingdom of God. Whatever it is, I believe that goals should be written, rather than merely thought or talked about. Habakkuk 2:2 says, "Record the vision and inscribe it on tablets, that the one who reads it may run."

A 1954 study of graduating seniors at Yale University showed that upon graduation, only 3 percent had written down specific, concrete goals. Twenty years later, this graduating class was surveyed again. The 3 percent that had developed the habit of writing down their goals had a cumulative wealth that was more than the other 97 percent combined.

You must write down your goals, or they will be nothing more than daydreams.

One of my mentors has a goal categorization system that he calls the Five Fs: faith, family, friends, finances, and fitness. Consider each area as you begin to set your goals.

Faith Goals
- *Spiritual:* church attendance, inspirational reading and study, contemplation and prayer time, service to others, relationship with clergy

Family Goals
- *Personal:* relationship with spouse, parents, children, other relatives; family priorities; family activities; changes in family routine of habits

Friends Goals
- *Social:* improve friendships, make new friends, become involved in club activities, seek out new recreational pursuits
- *Community:* volunteer work, civic clubs, political involvement, relationship with neighbors, community improvement activities

Financial Goals
- *Finances:* income, retirement fund, savings, investments, property, business capital, special funds, charitable giving
- *Professional:* promotion; participation in professional society; license or certification; continuing education; professional development activities; relationship with colleagues, superiors, subordinates, clients, vendors

Fitness Goals
- *Physical:* weight, level of fitness, nutrition plan, new sports skills, exercise schedule, makeover, dermatology, dentist, annual exam, wardrobe improvements
- *Mental:* nonfiction and fiction reading, self-education study, vocabulary-building exercises, enrollment in courses, cassette-tape courses

Remember that a goal is not a goal unless it has a deadline to it. In my seminars, I usually describe three kinds of goals:

1. *Short-term goals* can be achieved within three to six months.
2. *Intermediate goals* require six months to three years. They may include completing a college degree or vocational training program, reaching the middle-management level at your firm, or purchasing a new home.
3. *Long-range goals* take longer than three years. They include long-term career plans as well as things that you desire to do or be in future years for which you need to prepare now (like retirement).

3. Goals motivate you.

Again, the unrighteous steward in Luke 16 had a goal (to get a job), but what motivated him is found in verse 3: "I am not able to dig, and I am ashamed to beg" (AMP). The brother didn't want to get his hands dirty or ask anybody for help. He knew he could find a job, but he didn't want just any kind of job. He wanted a white-collar job instead of a blue-collar job. That was his motivation.

When I got married and had kids, that always served as a great financial motivation for me. I know it sounds crazy, but my business took a quantum leap upward after I got married and after each of my three kids was born. I wonder why. I believe it was because I loved my family, and I was motivated to provide for them. I didn't want my wife or my kids to have to suffer financially, so I began to work harder and smarter because I knew I had a wife and three kids to feed. Men, if you want to earn more money, here's the secret—get married and have lots of kids! It worked for me every time.

4. Goals proclaim God's will for your life.

To set a goal, if you are a Christian, you must believe that it is God's will for you to reach that goal. My good friend Ron Blue, in his book *Master Your Money*, said that a goal is a statement of God's will for you.

Goal Categorization Grid

Goals	Primary	Intermediate	Life
Physical			
Family			
Financial			
Professional			
Community			
Mental			
Social			
Spiritual			

The apostle Paul was probably one of the most goal-oriented men in the Bible. He said in Philippians 3:14, "I press on toward the goal for the prize of the upward call of God in Christ Jesus." Paul knew where he was going and why. His life was governed by his goal.

SEVEN OBSTACLES TO REACHING YOUR GOALS

1. Religious myths and old sayings

Through religious myths and old sayings, many people have been kept from their economic destiny. I know too many Christians that have incorrect attitudes and beliefs about money. Satan is the master deceiver, so he loves to provide us a steady flow of half-truths and distortions about money to keep us confused and broke. Satan will even use Scripture against you (in the wrong context, of course) to see if he can confuse you in the area of money. Without sugarcoating the truth, a lie would never be swallowed. Read Matthew 4:6 and see how Satan tried to use Scripture against Jesus.

See if you recognize any of these myths and fables:

- MYTH: Money is the root of all evil.
- REALITY: First Timothy 6:10 states that the *love* of money is the root of all sorts of evil, not money itself. Dr. Martin Luther King Jr. said it this way, "Jesus never made a sweeping indictment against wealth. Rather, He condemned the misuse of wealth. Money, like any other force such as electricity, is amoral and can be used for either good or evil."

- MYTH: It is hard for rich people to get into heaven.
- REALITY: The reason that it is hard for rich people to go to heaven isn't because God doesn't love rich people. The problem is that many who are rich don't love God. They simply have too much else to love already.

- MYTH: Poverty is a sign of spirituality.
- REALITY: God cares deeply for the poor, but this is out of His compassion—not their merit. Poverty is no more a sign of spirituality than wealth.

- MYTH: Jesus told a rich young ruler to sell his possessions and give his money away (Luke 18:18–22). Therefore, if you want to truly serve God, you shouldn't concern yourself with money. You will obtain your riches when you get to heaven.
- REALITY: Jesus' command to the rich young ruler was an individual surgery; He was not setting forth a universal diagnosis. Having evaluated the state of his heart, Christ issued the specific diagnosis He knew was necessary and best for this specific man.

- MYTH: Jesus was poor and had nowhere to lay His head (Matthew 8:20); therefore, if we want to be like Jesus, we should be poor, too.

- REALITY: When you own not only the cattle on a thousand hills but also the hills themselves, you aren't poor. Jesus became poor, in order that through His poverty we might be rich (2 Corinthians 8:9). He was poor for a reason, and a season. Furthermore, Jesus and the disciples did have money; they weren't exactly poverty-stricken. They had a treasurer and many of the disciples left successful businesses to follow Jesus.

- MYTH: Jesus said that you can't serve God and money (Luke16:13).
- REALITY: That's right; you can't *serve* God and money, but you can *have* God and money. I can have more than one brother, sister, friend, or more than one job, but I can only have one wife. Some relationships are exclusive in nature. It's the same with our relationship with God. Either He is on the throne or money is, but both cannot be on the throne together.

- MYTH: All preachers want is your money.
- REALITY: In the day of the megachurch and the TV pastor, we sometimes forget that most Black churches are not wealthy institutions. Close to half of the Black clergy nationwide (45.1 percent) must work at another full-time occupation in order to support themselves.[2] Remember that Satan is the master of extremes. He is delighted when pastors are underpaid and underappreciated and just as delighted when they are overpaid and overappreciated. Always keep in mind 1 Timothy 5:18, "You shall not muzzle an ox when it is treading out the grain, and . . . the laborer is worthy of his hire" (AMP)

- MYTH: When a person tithes and gives, God will automatically meet all of that person's needs and desires regardless of what he does with the rest of his money.
- REALITY: What you do with the tithe (10 percent of your gross income) does not negate what you should do with the other 90 percent. God is interested in your being a good steward with the entire amount, not just the 10 percent.

- MYTH: I need to drive a nice car, live in a big house, and wear designer clothes, so I can be a better witness for Christ.
- REALITY: Jesus doesn't say that by your BMW, by your address, or by your clothes that all men shall know that you are His disciples. He said that it would be our love toward one another, not our fabulous material possessions, that will exemplify our Christlikeness (John 13:35).

- MYTH: If God is blessing you financially, you must be living right; and if you are struggling financially, something must be wrong with your walk with God.
- REALITY: This "do good and you'll be well-off, and do bad and you won't" mentality is another half-truth. Wealth is not a sign of God's approval, no more than financial adversity is a sign of His disapproval. Sometimes the righteous do suffer, and those who are evil don't. But don't put God in a box. Yes, there are benefits to living right, and there are consequences to sin, but don't judge a person's spiritual life by the things that he does or does not possess.

2. Fear of failure

Many people, especially Black folks, would have and could have done some incredible things if it weren't for the fear of failure. Too many of us have become afraid to dream big and are reluctant to express a desire for something greater than what is available in our social circle for fear of being looked upon as being too ambitious or greedy. Actually, the fear of failure is more like the fear of "what will they say if I mess up?" The only way to avoid failure at all costs is to do nothing. Although you avoid failure and defeat by doing nothing, you also avoid success and fulfillment.

My very first attempt in the investment business was a complete, utter failure. As a matter of fact, the first investment firm I ever worked for fired me after three months! I didn't do anything wrong, but I did fail to meet their minimum requirements. The branch manager who fired me told me that I was not cut out for the investment business, and I ought to try something else. Well, fifteen years later, the same firm that fired me has offered me close to $1 million, up front, to come and join their firm! Isn't it ironic? Fifteen years ago they fired me; now they think I'm the greatest thing since sliced bread. That's why you have to be careful whom you listen to. You can't let what people say or don't say about you determine your destiny. I never gave up on my dream even though I failed the first time. Remember this: If you do fail—and we all do—let failure be your teacher and not your undertaker.

3. *Being intimidated by time*

Many people who don't set goals feel it's too late for them, or that the goals they desire will take too long, or that they are too old. Never think like that. If you feel like you need to go back to school, get in shape, save money, or invest in the stock market, then do it! It's never too late to start.

Always keep improving and setting goals no matter how old you are. Colonel Sanders, the founder of Kentucky Fried Chicken, and Mary Kay Ashe, the founder of Mary Kay Cosmetics, were both well over fifty years old when they started their business careers. Now both of their companies are billion-dollar companies. Remember this: you are never too old to be what you could have been.

4. *Low self-esteem*

So many African-Americans feel they don't deserve a better life financially. African-Americans have such a strong historical identity with poverty and lack that we sometimes struggle with whether we deserve success. If you don't see yourself as being worthy of financial success, you will never pursue it. If you don't think you deserve that $70,000-a-year job, then you'll never get it.

Do you know that how you feel about yourself can nullify the plans that God has for you? In Numbers 13, Moses sent out some spies to check out the land that God had promised the children of Israel. It was their land; God told them it was their land. However, when the spies saw giants in the land, they got scared and never took hold of what God had ordained for them. They saw themselves as grasshoppers instead of giant slayers. God never saw them as grasshoppers, but that's how they saw themselves. Consequently, they never reached their promised land.

If you conclude that your self-esteem is low, I heartily recommend that you set as your number one goal to "develop better self-esteem." Make it a priority in your life.

5. Not thinking big enough

The most dangerous attitude that hinders people from reaching their goal is thinking too small. Many people simply can't comprehend having a million dollars, or even $100,000, for that matter. Too many African-Americans are satisfied with just "making it," or just "getting by," instead of striving to have more than enough. Many are content with having just enough or just making ends meet. This kind of attitude simply reflects what you think about yourself.

Perhaps the greatest torture that could be devised would be for us to be forced in our later years to watch a videotape of the life we could have led had we dared to believe in and pursue the dreams and goals that were available and attainable in our lifetimes. Don't create your own limitations; think big!

6. Unrealistic goals

I was very apprehensive about even adding this as an obstacle, because most of the people I know think too small, especially Christians. But every now and then, people come up to me with their "pie in the sky" dreams, and deep inside I know they aren't ready. I never want to destroy someone's dream or burst his bubble, and I don't, but I must point out to folks that million-dollar dreams require a blueprint. You can't build a million-dollar house without a blueprint, and neither can you build a million-dollar business without much planning, sacrifice, and hard work. You must be realistic first, and then ask God for wisdom so your plans will be established.

7. Unwillingness to change

If you want your financial situation to be different, then you must be willing to change. A friend of mine has a saying: "If you want to continue getting what you are getting, just keep doing what you've been doing." You can't expect your life to change if you don't. Insanity is doing the same thing over and over and expecting different results. Are you suffering from financial insanity?

Author Dennis Waitley in his book *Timing Is Everything* described a research project that someone did about a native tribe in South America. The people in the tribe had been dying prematurely from a strange illness for many generations. Scientists finally discovered that an insect that lived in the walls of their adobe homes carried the disease. The natives faced several possible solutions. They could destroy the insects with a pesticide, tear down and rebuild their homes, move to another location where those insects weren't found. . . . or they could do nothing and continue to die young, just as they had for generations. What did they choose to do? Incredibly, they chose to remain as they were. They took the path of least resistance and no change.

Many people I meet have a similar attitude when it comes to their finances. They realize if they do certain things, they can succeed. The things require change, however, and they resist the change. Don't allow yourself to stay as you are and die without ever reaching your financial goals.

HOW TO SET GOALS

The art of goal-setting is a simple process. The first thing we must believe is that God has a plan for us and that He wants to accomplish great things in us. Then we have to be available, not necessarily able, for God to use us. Setting goals is a four-step process.

1. Spend time with God.

If you spent as much time with God as you do eating, what type of spiritual life would you have? Think about it. Most of us find the time to eat three square meals a day but struggle to find the time to spend with God. If eating food regularly can impact our bodies, then spending time with God (eating spiritual food) can greatly impact our spiritual lives. The time we spend with God also has financial implications.

> This book of the law shall not depart from your mouth, but you shall meditate on it day and night, so that you may be careful to do according to all that is written in it; for then you will make your way prosperous, and then you will have success. (Joshua 1:8)

> How blessed is the man who does not walk in the counsel of the wicked, nor stand in the path of sinners, nor sit in the seat of scoffers! But his delight is in the law of the Lord, and in His law he meditates day and night. He will be like a tree firmly planted by streams of water, which yields its fruit in its season and its leaf does not wither; and in whatever he does, he prospers. (Psalm 1:1–3)

Spending time with God is essential; otherwise, goal setting without God's direction becomes merely the striving after your own imagination and dreams. Don't forget that a goal is a statement of God's will for your life.

2. Write down the impressions.

As you spend time with God, you need to write down what you believe He is saying to you. I have found that over time, as you write down the impressions, you will receive the assurance and conviction to step out in faith and do what God is calling you to do. I enjoy looking back on some of my journaling notes of the time I spent with God and seeing what He's done in my life. It's incredible how much you can accomplish when you are directed by the Holy Spirit.

3. Make the goal measurable.

After spending time with the Lord and writing down your impressions of what He seems to be saying, you are ready to set real goals. Because goals are measurable, we know definitely when they have been achieved.

4. Just do it!

James 2:17 states that faith without works is dead. All the planning in the world is no substitute for just doing it! Faith is like a muscle—you get it stronger by exercising it. Faith is also an action word, and it's about stepping out on what God wants you to do and going for it. Don't just stick your foot in the water—dive in!

At this point, you know where you are, and you know what God would have you to do financially. The next step is to begin the action steps to accomplish the goals that God has given you. Remember, you don't have to see *how*. You may not have the resources yet, but you can take action.

Dr. Benjamin E. Mays, scholar, educator, and president emeritus of Morehouse College, put it succinctly: "It must be borne in the mind that the great tragedy of life doesn't lie in not reaching your goal. The tragedy lies in having no goal to reach. It isn't calamity to die with dreams unfulfilled, but it is a calamity not to dream. It is not a disaster to be unable to capture your ideal, but it is a disaster to have no ideal to capture. It is not a disgrace not to reach the stars, but it is a disgrace to have no stars to reach for. Not failure, but low aim is sin."

Chapter Four

FROM FINANCIAL BONDAGE TO FREEDOM

talk to me about their finances.
d were deacons in the church.
$110,000. With only one child,
ut four nights a week, Caribbean
s. Whatever they wanted, they
g session, I let the wife talk first.
se and have another child," Joan
gage, we were turned down be-
ad been late making credit-card
aved."
ed. Company restructuring cost
d to support the family's extrav-
Although David found a new po-
ssed payments threw an already

ed to pay one credit card with

S

the other," Joan said. "We had charged some of the vacations and dinners on the credit cards and never really paid off the entire amount when the bill came. So our balances were very high. We owed more than $24,000 in credit-card debt alone. We had to let one of the cars go and got behind in all our bills, including our mortgage. I thought we were going to lose the house." Then Joan started to cry. "The one thing I wanted most had to be delayed. There is no way I can take time off to have another baby."

Then there's the story of Malik Harrison. "I hated to hear the phone ring," says the thirty-one-year-old husband, father, and salesperson. "I was afraid it was one of my creditors with a demand for money. I even learned how to disguise my voice when they called. In the meantime, my bills were sitting in the drawer unpaid. I have little or nothing to show for the debt, and I am employed in a job that I hate, just to keep up the payments." How did Malik wind up in this situation? "I did not build up this huge debt by living an extravagant life. I did like most people do, one charge at a time for little things that my salary could not handle. And there were the occasional big-ticket items like the car-repair bills and an expensive prescription not covered by insurance. After years of mostly paying minimum balances and continuous charging, I owed my creditors $21,000."

SLAVES TO DEBT

The situations for Joan and David and Malik are very different, yet they are the same. Joan and David got into their situation through extravagance, Malik through small purchases over time. Regardless of how they got there, they are all slaves to debt. You see, the Emancipation Proclamation did not free the slaves. Only the color of slavery has changed. Instead of Whites enslaving Blacks, now we have green (the color of money) enslaving Red, Yellow, Black, and White! No matter what race, creed, or color you may be, debt is a form of slavery that has many of us in bondage.

Personal debt is everywhere in America. Twenty million Americans are overwhelmed by it at this very moment, many only a paycheck or two ahead of bankruptcy, and millions more are living in daily stress because of it. Debt has now reached a level where 23 percent of the average person's take-home pay is already committed to payments on existing debt, not including the home mortgage! With all this credit floating around, we have serious financial casualties. In 1998 more than 1,400,000 individuals filed for bankruptcy in our country, more bankruptcies than during the Great Depression.

Because of increased accessibility to credit, more and more African-American families are burdened by credit-card debts. It seems that we are more easily swayed by slick advertising that tells us to spend, spend, spend. This do-it-now, pay-for-it-later mentality has gotten many of us in some serious trouble. *For many of us, our status symbols have become our shackles.* What's so alarming about African-Americans and debt is that the credit industry makes it so easy for us to get loans for cars, consumer products, furniture, etc.—things that depreciate in value—but it's often difficult for us to get business loans and mortgages—things that increase our net worth. Something is wrong with that picture. Far too many of us are overextended in our credit and undercapitalized in our businesses. That's why we have to take responsibility and educate ourselves about debt.

Historically, individuals and institutions have misled many African-Americans when it comes to credit and debt. Southern Blacks, especially, were exploited and kept in perpetual debt by Whites who kept them working in cotton fields in systems known as sharecropping and tenant farming. This abuse even followed Blacks as they moved up North with low down-payment plans, high-interest financing, dishonest used-car operations, and rent-to-own operations. Today, the practice of giving easy credit to families who are unprepared to handle credit is widespread in the Black community. Companies are so successful in enticing African-Americans to use credit that the African-American share of the national indebtedness far outpaces its percentage of the population. Overall, 68.5 percent of African-American families are in debt for mortgages, home equity loans, installment payments, credit cards, and other debt.[1]

As men and women of God, it is imperative that we move from financial bondage to financial freedom. There is a greater need to reduce and eliminate our debt in order to have resources to invest wisely and strate-gically in the kingdom of God, and for our families and future generations.

DEFINING DEBT

The dictionary defines *debt* as money which one person is obligated to pay to another. Debt includes money owed to credit-card companies, bank loans, student loans, money borrowed from relatives, mortgages, and past-due medical bills. Bills that come due, such as the monthly phone bill, are not considered debt if they are paid on time.

THE REAL COST OF DEBT

We all need to understand the cost of debt. Debt imposes a finan-cial, physical, and generational cost. Assume you have $5,560 in cred-it-card debt at an 18 percent interest rate. This would cost you about $1,000 in interest annually. This is compound interest in reverse. Study the chart below.

What Does Debt Really Cost?

	Year 5	Year 10	Year 20	Year 30	Year 40
Amount of of interest you paid:	$5,000	$10,000	$20,000	$30,000	$40,000
What you would earn on the $1,000 invested at the 12 percent:	6,353	17,549	72,052	214,333	767,091
How much the lender earns from your payment at 18 percent interest:	7,154	23,521	146,628	790,948	4,163,213

You can see what lenders have known for a long time—the incredible impact of compounding interest working against you and for them. The lender will accumulate a total of $4,163,213 if you pay him $1,000 a year for forty years, and he earns 18 percent on your payment! Is there any wonder credit-card companies are eager for you to become one of their borrowers? It is big business for them and very profitable.

Now compare the $40,000 you paid in interest over forty years with the $767,091 you could have accumulated, earning 12 percent on $1,000 invested each year: $767,091 yields a monthly income of $7,671 if it's earning 12 percent, without ever touching the principal.

Stop to consider this: When a person assumes debt of $5,560 and pays $1,000 a year in interest when he could earn 12 percent in an investment instead, he actually costs himself $767,091 over forty years. Debt has a much higher cost than many realize. Next time you are tempted to purchase something with credit cards, ask yourself if the long-term benefits of staying out of debt outweigh the short-term benefits of the purchase.

Debt also often increases stress, which contributes to mental, physical, and emotional fatigue. It can harm relationships. Many people raise their lifestyle through debt, only to discover that the burden of debt then controls their lifestyle. Every dollar they earn that is not spent on basic needs is turned over to a creditor. This is a new form of slavery, where the chains of debt keep people trapped in a life of worry, hopelessness, and despair. People have become financial slaves, working for lenders rather than for themselves. The bumper sticker that reads, "I owe, I owe, it's off to work I go," is an unfortunate reality for too many people.

Lastly, many people are in so much debt that they are robbing the financial future of their children to support an extravagant lifestyle. This is the ultimate form of selfishness, and I see it all the time. I'm always amazed at people who will sacrifice to get the luxury car of their dreams but won't sacrifice to save for their children's college education. The Bible says, "Where your treasure is, there your heart will be also" (Luke 12:34). In other words, you can find out what a man truly loves by where he spends his money. I wonder sometimes what our spending habits say about how much we love our kids. Parents should be laying up money for the next generation, not just indulging themselves on their own wants and desires.

DEBT IN SCRIPTURE

Scripture's perspective of debt is clear. Carefully read the first portion of Romans 13:8 from several different Bible translations: "Owe no man any thing" (KJV). "Let no debt remain outstanding" (NIV). "Pay all your debts" (TLB). "Owe nothing to anyone" (NASB). "Keep out of debt and owe no man anything" (AMP).

1. Debt is slavery.

In Proverbs 22:7 we learn why our Lord speaks so directly to the area of debt: "Just as the rich rule the poor, so the borrower is servant to the lender" (TLB). When we are in debt, we are in a position of servitude to the lender. And the deeper we are in debt, the more of a servant we become. To be more direct, we become like slaves. We do not have the freedom to decide where to spend our income, because our money is already legally obligated to meet these debts.

In 1 Corinthians 7:23 Paul writes, "You were bought with a price; do not become slaves of men." Our Father made the ultimate sacrifice by giving His Son, the Lord Jesus Christ, to die for us. And He now wants His children free to serve Him, and not people, in whatever way He chooses.

2. Debt was considered a curse.

In the Old Testament, being out of debt was one of the promised rewards for obedience.

> Now it shall be, if you will diligently obey the Lord your God, being careful to do all His commandments which I command you today, the Lord your God will set you high above all the nations of the earth. All these blessings shall come upon you and overtake you if you obey

the Lord your God . . . and you shall lend to many nations, but you shall not borrow. (Deuteronomy 28:1–2, 12)

However, indebtedness was one of the curses inflicted for disobedience.

> But it shall come about, if you will not obey the Lord your God, to observe to do all His commandments and His statutes with which I charge you today, that all these curses shall come upon you and overtake you. . . . The alien who is among you shall rise above you higher and higher, but you shall go down lower and lower. He shall lend to you, but you shall not lend to him; he shall be the head, and you shall be the tail. (Deuteronomy 28:15, 43–44)

3. *Debt presumes upon tomorrow.*

When we get into debt, we assume that we will earn enough in the future to pay the debt. Scripture cautions us against presumption: "Come now, you who say, 'Today or tomorrow we will go to such and such a city, and spend a year there and engage in business and make a profit.' Yet you do not know what your life will be like tomorrow. You are just a vapor that appears for a little while and then vanishes away. Instead, you ought to say, 'If the Lord wills, we will live and also do this or that'" (James 4:13–15).

4. *Debt may deny God an opportunity.*

A newlywed couple asked me for financial advice. They were excited about their new apartment. They had some old furniture from their single days, but they wanted to furnish the apartment with new furniture and did not have the money to do it. The only way they could afford to buy more furniture was to use credit cards. However, that would put added financial pressure on them because they already had two car notes and school loans. They agreed to trust the Lord to provide instead of incurring more debt. Within six months, God provided furniture for their entire apartment through an elderly couple who was moving and wanted to give away some of their furniture. The furniture was slightly used but more stylish and of better quality than the set they were thinking about purchasing—and best of all, it was *free!* Borrowing may deny God an opportunity to demonstrate His reality.

THE "PROBLEM DEBT" QUIZ

As a general rule, your monthly debt obligations should not exceed 35 percent of your gross monthly income. If you owe more than that, you are flirting with trouble. There are other guidelines you can use. Ask yourself the questions on the following checklist. One or more "yes" answers may indicate that you have debt problems.

1. Do you only have enough money to pay the minimum balance amount on your credit-card statements each month?
2. Are any of your installment loans past due?
3. Are your credit cards at the limit?
4. Are you unable to pay real estate taxes, insurance bills, or other infrequent expenses from your current income?
5. Do you currently "rotate" payments to creditors, paying one this month but not the next?
6. Do you rely on overtime or a second job in order to pay bills?
7. Have you ever had a charge refused because your account had been suspended or because there was insufficient credit available?

TAKING OUT A LOAN

Scripture is silent on the subject of when we can owe money. In my opinion, there is such a thing as smart debt and dumb debt, even though the best kind of debt is no debt! I believe there are a few debts that could possibly qualify as smart debts: money owed for a home mortgage, for your business, or for your vocation. This is permissible, I believe, only if the following three criteria are met:

1. The item purchased is an asset with the potential to appreciate or produce an income.

2. The value of the item equals or exceeds the amount owed against it.
3. The debt should not be so high that repayment puts undue strain on the budget.

Let me give you an example of how a home mortgage might qualify. Historically, the home has usually been an appreciating asset, so it meets the first criterion. If you invest a reasonable down payment, you could expect to sell the home for at least enough to satisfy the mortgage, and this meets the second requirement. Lastly, the monthly house payment should not strain your budget.

If you meet all the criteria and assume some "possible debt," I pray you will immediately establish the goal of eliminating even this debt. There is no assurance that the housing market will appreciate or even maintain current values. A loss of job can interrupt your income. Please consider trying to pay off all debt.

NINE STEPS TO FINANCIAL FREEDOM

Our family's goal is to become absolutely debt-free, even from our home mortgage. When I share my personal goal with my seminar audiences, someone always asks me, "Brother Lee, isn't it smarter to keep your money invested in the market and earn 10 to 20 percent than to pay off a 7 percent mortgage? And what about the tax write-off—why forgo that?" My answer is always the same. First of all, you have to do what you believe the Lord is leading you to do for your family. Second, there is no guarantee that you'll make 10 to 20 percent in the stock market. And third, paying off a mortgage may not make economic sense, but it certainly makes emotional sense. When you own something, nobody can take it from you. I always rate "peace of mind" advantages right up there with financial advantages. Therefore, I believe the goal for most of us should be D-Day, "Debtless Day," when you become absolutely free of debt. Many feel this is impossible, but I know hundreds of people who make an average income who are now debt-free. Most of them paid off their credit cards and some even their mortgages. With God's help, you can do this too.

Here are nine steps for getting out of debt. The steps are simple, but following them requires hard work.

1. Pray for the Lord's help.

In 2 Kings 4:1–7, a widow was threatened with losing her children to her creditor, and she appealed to the prophet Elisha for help. Elisha instructed the widow to borrow many empty jars from her neighbors. The Lord multiplied her only possession, a small quantity of oil, and all the jars were filled. She sold the increased oil and paid her debts to free her children. The same God who provided for the widow is interested in you becoming free of debt.

2. Establish a written budget.

In my experience, few people in debt have been using a written budget. Most people just wing it! They may have had a budget neatly filed away in a drawer, but they have not been using it. A written budget helps you plan ahead, analyze your spending patterns, and control the biggest budget buster of them all—impulse spending.

3. List everything you own.

Evaluate your assets to determine if there is anything you do not need that might be sold to help you get out of debt more quickly. How about that set of golf clubs gathering dust? Or that expensive car that can be sold and replaced with a more affordable one? What other assets can you sell that will help you get out of debt?

4. List everything you owe.

Many people, particularly if they owe a lot of money, do not know exactly what they owe. List your debts to determine your current financial situation. You also need to determine the interest rate your creditors are charging for each debt.

Debt List

Date: _____

Creditor	Describe What Was Purchased	Monthly Payments	Balance Due	Scheduled Pay Off Date	Interest Rate	Payments Past Due
Totals						

Auto Loans						
Total Auto Loans						

Home Mortgages						
Total Home Mortgages						

Business/Investment Debt						
Total Business/Investment Debt						

Debt Repayment Schedule

Creditor: _____ Date: _____

Describe What Was Purchased: _____

Amount Owed: _____ Interest Rate: _____

Date Due:	Amount	Payments Remaining	Balance Due

5. Establish a debt repayment schedule.

I also recommend that you establish a repayment schedule for each debt. I suggest you decide which debts to pay off first based on two factors:

- *Pay off small debts.* Focus on paying off the smallest debts first. You will be encouraged as they are eliminated, and this will free up cash to apply against other debts. After you pay off the first debt, apply its payment toward the next debt you wish to retire. After the second debt is paid off, apply what you were paying on the first and second debts toward the next debt you wish to eliminate, and so forth.

- *Pay off higher interest rate debts.* Determine what rate of interest you are being charged on each debt, and try to first pay off those that charge the highest rate. If you call your credit-card company to set up an accelerated debt payment schedule, you may be able to negotiate a reduced interest rate.

6. Consider earning additional income.

Many people hold jobs that simply do not produce enough income to meet their needs, even if they spend wisely. If you earn additional income, decide in advance to pay off debts with the added earnings. We tend to spend more than we make, whether we earn a little or a lot. Spending always seems to keep ahead of earning, so do not fall into the trap of spending all the extra income that you make.

7. Control the use of credit cards.

A wave of 2.5 billion solicitations a year offering credit cards is overwhelming our mailboxes. Many of these solicitations are deceptive, promising low interest rates, which in the fine print rise to very high levels within a few months. Experts say debt is skyrocketing because credit has become increasingly available. I do not believe that credit cards are sinful, but they are extremely dangerous. It is estimated that people carry more than 800,000,000 credit cards, and only 40 percent of them are paid in full each month. People spend approximately one-third more when they use credit cards rather than cash, because they feel they are not really spending money (because it's just plastic). As one shopper said to another, "I like credit cards lots more than money, because they go so much farther!" When I look at the finances of someone in debt, I use a simple rule of thumb to determine whether credit cards are too dangerous for them. If they do not pay the entire balance due at the end of each month, I encourage them to perform some plastic surgery—any good scissors will do.

8. *Be content with what you have.*

The advertising industry uses powerful methods to get consumers to buy. Frequently, the message is intended to create discontent with what we have.

A clear example is the American company that opened a new plant in Central America because the labor was plentiful and inexpensive. Everything went well until the villagers received their first paycheck; afterward they did not return to work. Several days later, the manager went down to the village chief to determine the cause of this problem. The chief responded, "Why should we work? We already have everything we need." The plant stood idle for two months until someone came up with the bright idea of sending a mail-order catalog to every villager. There has never been an employment problem since!

Note these three realities of our consumer-driven society:

- The more television you watch, the more you spend.
- The more you look at catalogs and magazines, the more you spend.
- The more you shop, the more you spend.

9. *Do not give up!*

The last step is the most difficult one in getting out of debt. It takes hard work. Here are three things you must do: Stop spending more than you make; pay interest on the debt; and pay back what you owe.

It is never easy to get out of debt, but the freedom is worth the struggle.

Remember, there has always been a price to pay for our freedom.

ESCAPING THE AUTO DEBT TRAP

Automobile loans are one of the leading causes of indebtedness. According to a recent Black investor survey, affluent African-Americans spend more on car payments than they invest in their children's education. Even when I drive through low-income areas in Atlanta, some of the people who are the so-called "poor" have nicer cars than I do!

It seems that Black Americans have always had a love affair with wheels. In the African-American community, a luxury car is the ultimate status symbol, signifying that one has arrived and is going places. According to Earl Graves Jr., president and chief operating officer of *Black Enterprise* magazine, Blacks on average are six times more likely than Whites to buy a Mercedes, and the average income of a Black who buys a Jaguar is about one-third less than that of a White purchaser of the luxury vehicle. That's because automobile leases have made it easier for just about anybody to drive in style. All you need is a small down payment and enough income to pay the $500 to $1,500 monthly notes, and you can look like "Mr. Big Stuff." But as the song says, "Who do you think you are?" You're certainly not wealthy or prosperous just because you have a nice ride. Some of us are literally driving ourselves to the poorhouse. Unfortunately, this ego-driven conspicuous consumption is occurring at our children's expense.

I fell into the same luxury-car-buying trap as a young businessman in the early 1990s. As soon as my income exceeded $100,000, the very first thing I did was to go buy me a brand-spanking-new Mercedes Benz. Now, there is nothing wrong with a new car or a Mercedes Benz. It's an incredible automobile. However, my motivation to buy the car was not because it was a great automobile but to show the world that I had arrived! I was making a little money, and I wanted everybody to know it! Eventually, I ended up selling the car because God started dealing with me about my stewardship, my children's future, and getting out of debt. I sensed the Lord simply saying to me, "Lee, do you want to look wealthy or be wealthy?" I ended up buying a pre-owned car that I paid off, and used the extra savings to invest in the stock market and to give to the kingdom.

Seventy percent of all automobiles are financed. The average person keeps his car between three and four years. The average car lasts for twelve years. Here's how to escape this trap. First of all, realize that new cars lose up to 60 percent of their value in the first three years, so consider buying used ones. Second, decide in advance to keep your car for at least five years. Third, pay off your automobile loan. Finally, continue paying the monthly car payment, but pay it to yourself into a savings account. Then when you are ready to replace your car, the saved cash plus the trade-in should be sufficient to buy your car without credit. It may not be a new car, but you should be able to purchase a good, low-mileage used car without any debt.

YOUR RESPONSIBILITIES TO REPAY YOUR DEBT

Many wait to make payments to the creditors until their payments are past due, even when they have the money. Some of us have become experts at robbing Peter and making Paul wait. This, however, is not biblical. "Do not withhold good from those to whom it is due, when it is in your power to do it. Do not say to your neighbor, 'Go, and come back, and tomorrow I will give it,' when you have it with you" (Proverbs 3:27–28).

Godly people should pay their debts and bills as promptly as they can. Always being a day late and a dollar short does not demonstrate to others that knowing Jesus Christ has made us responsible.

USING YOUR SAVINGS

A lot of people in my seminars ask me if it is wise to use all your savings to pay off debt. My answer is that it is wise to maintain a reasonable level of savings to provide for the unexpected. If you apply all

your savings against debt and the unexpected does occur, you will probably be forced to incur more debt to fund the emergency. The reason
a lot of people are in debt is because of inadequate cash reserves.

BANKRUPTCY: THE LAST RESORT

A court can declare a person bankrupt and unable to pay his debts.
Depending upon the type of bankruptcy, the court will either allow
the debtor to develop a plan to repay his creditors, or the court will
distribute his property among the creditors as payment for the debts.
A wave of bankruptcy is sweeping our country. I have counseled many
people who asked me the question, "Should a godly person declare
bankruptcy?" The answer is generally no. Psalm 37:21 tells us, "The
wicked borrows and does not pay back, but the righteous is gracious and
gives." In my opinion, bankruptcy is permissible under two circumstances: A creditor forces a person into bankruptcy, or counselors believe the debtor's emotional health is at stake because of inability to cope
with the pressure of unreasonable creditors.

After a person goes through bankruptcy, he should seek counsel
from an attorney to determine if it's legal to attempt to repay the debt
when he is not obligated to do so. If it is within the law, he should
make every effort to repay the debt. For a large debt, this may be a long-
term goal that is largely dependent upon the Lord's supernatural provision.

CO-SIGNING

Co-signing relates to debt. Anytime you co-sign, you become legally responsible for the debt of another. It is just as if you went to the bank,
borrowed the money, and gave it to your friend or relative who is asking you to co-sign.

A Federal Trade Commission study found that 50 percent of those
who co-signed for bank loans ended up having to make the payment
themselves. Seventy-five percent of those who co-signed for finance
company loans ended up making the payments! Unfortunately, few co-

signers plan for default. The casualty rate is so high because the professional lender has already determined that the loan is a bad risk. That is why he won't make the loan without someone who is financially responsible to guarantee its repayment. Fortunately, Scripture speaks very clearly about co-signing. Proverbs 17:18 reads, "It is poor judgment to countersign another's note, to become responsible for his debts" (TLB). The words "poor judgment" are better translated "destitute of mind"! Please use sound judgment and never co-sign a note or become surety for any debt, unless you are able and willing to make the payments yourself.

HOME MORTGAGES

A thirty-year home mortgage, at a 10 percent interest rate, will require you to pay more than three times the amount originally borrowed. If you own a home or plan to purchase one in the future, I would like to encourage you to pay it off more rapidly than it is scheduled. When my wife and I first began to understand God's financial principles, we decided to work toward paying off everything, including the home mortgage. We began to explore how we might accomplish this. Let's examine the payment schedule for a home mortgage. Please do not let the size of the mortgage or the rate of interest hinder you; this is for illustration only. In the chart on the next page, we are assuming a $75,000 mortgage at a 12 percent interest rate, paid over thirty years. The first year of the payment schedule would look like the chart. As you can see, the payments during the early years are almost all interest. Out of the total of $9,257.64 in house payments made this first year, only $272.26 went toward principal reduction! In fact, it will be $23\frac{1}{2}$ years before the principal and the interest portions of the payment equal each other! I don't know about you, but a thirty-year goal to pay off my home mortgage doesn't excite me. There are several methods we can use to pay off the mortgage in half the time.

One method is to increase the amount of your monthly payment. In our example, a $75,000 mortgage at 12 percent interest payable over thirty years requires a monthly installment of $771.47. If you increase the monthly payment by $128.70 to $900.17, the mortgage will be fully paid in fifteen years. You will save $138,864 in interest over the life of your mortgage. A second method is to prepay the next month's principal payment in addition to your regular monthly payment of $771.47. By doing this consistently for fifteen years, you will have paid off the entire mortgage. During the early years, the additional principal payment is low, but in the later years the extra payment will become much larger.

Let your lender know what you are planning. Not many borrowers prepay their mortgages, so he may be in shock for a while!

Home Mortgage

Original mortgage amount	$100,000.00
Monthly mortgage payment at 10 percent interest	$877.57
Months paid	x360
Total payments	$315,925.20

CREDIT AND YOU

Mortgage lender Freddie Mac conducted a survey recently that revealed 30 percent of Americans have bad credit. Mac's survey also said that 47 percent of Blacks and 34 percent of Hispanics have bad credit. Among Whites surveyed, 27 percent have bad credit. Consumers were judged to have "bad credit" if they had been either ninety days late on a payment in the last two years or thirty days late on a payment more than once in the last two years, or have a record of delinquent liens, unpaid taxes on property, or bankruptcy. The study found that while bad credit crosses racial and economic lines, it is pervasive among Blacks.

Let me set the record straight: Just because a person has bad credit doesn't mean that he is a deadbeat or someone not to be trusted. Most people, at the time they incur debt, fully intend to honor their responsibility to repay what they owe. If you are normally a responsible person but are falling behind on your bills, the first step toward fiscal rehabilitation is to contact your creditors. Work out agreements with them that allow you to make smaller payments until things improve. Most credit-card companies will be glad to make this arrangement. It's best to take this step as soon as you begin to fall behind in your payments, before too many blemishes appear on your credit report.

The second step is to put yourself on a strict budget so that overspending is curbed. The third step is to write or call a credit bureau and order a copy of your credit report. The report will show how many negative reports are on your records. Your credit report is the history of the way you pay your bills. If an account has been referred to a collection agency, if you have defaulted on credit agreements or loans, if there are judgments against you, if you have declared bankruptcy, or if liens have been recorded against your property, this information will be on your report. It will also show late payments on credit cards. The fourth step is to not apply for new credit until your report has been cleaned up. Whenever you apply for new credit and get rejected, your declined application goes on your report for two years. Take care of your business first. Then think hard before adding to your debt.

Chapter Five

FINDING PURPOSE
IN YOUR WORK

$\mathcal{S}$. B. Fuller could hardly contain his excitement. He had seen what all entrepreneurs call a "window of opportunity," and he was determined to pry it open. He rushed to Dr. King's makeshift offices in downtown Montgomery and exclaimed, "Martin, we've won—the boycott has worked. No one is riding the bus!" For nearly a century, local Whites had controlled Montgomery, Alabama, an economic mecca during the 1950s. From this cradle of Confederacy, a wellspring of business activity and prosperity flourished that included iron, textiles, and transportation, while half of its inhabitants suffered physical and economic abuse. By 1957, a young Baptist minister from neighboring Atlanta, Georgia, Martin Luther King Jr., was vaulted into national prominence when he sought to correct a host of injustices. Thus, the Montgomery Bus Boycott was born. Dr. King's stride toward freedom carried a message that Black America openly embraced. Thanks, in part, to his urging, fifty thousand Negroes were willing to substitute tired feet for tired souls and walk the streets of Montgomery until the walls of segregation were finally battered by the forces of justice.

In short order, the boycott took its effect, and the numbers did not go unnoticed. For months, Fuller, an astute businessman who was twice King's age with a net worth in the millions, studied bus routes, city maps, and the records of comparable Northern carriers. Black patrons—the city's largest consumer group—had made their point. The savvy tycoon saw an enterprise on its knees in a tight money pinch, and he stood ready to solve the firm's problem in a manner he knew best. All Fuller had to do was to follow up his hunch with hard numbers, sales, and expense projections, and sell his idea to King and his staff. A piece of cake? Hardly.

With data in hand, Fuller ran up the steps leading to the pastor's study, blurting out, "Martin, we've got them just where we want them. The city has got to sell!"

King sat back, shocked, without the slightest idea what his visitor was talking about. Without stopping to catch his breath, Fuller continued, "Man, I've looked at this thing from every possible angle, and I'm telling you, the bus line is hurting. Go ask A. G." A. G., of course, was Arthur G. Gaston, the Black insurance and banking whiz—and master visionary. Gaston took a liking to Fuller's bold plans. "We know they've got to sell," he said. "We'll call Atlanta and Chicago, put the finances together, and buy them out. Then we can drive the bus anywhere we please!" Unfortunately, in the late 1950s, economic empowerment was not the focus of the struggle. At this critical juncture in history, Black leadership said, "But . . ."[1]

I am so thankful for the leadership of Dr. Martin Luther King Jr. and the bravery of Rosa Parks and the many others who literally gave their lives for the freedoms we now take for granted. Without them I would not be where I am today.

However, as a businessman, I do regret that during the Montgomery Bus Boycott of 1955 we didn't realize that after 381 days of creating an alternative bus system, we could have created our own.

I grew up in the South, and my grandparents' goal was to ride on a bus. My parents' goal was to sit in the front of a bus. Today my goal would be to own the bus company! Creating new jobs is a top economic priority for the African-American culture. The mantra in the 1950s and

1960s was "Get a good education, then get a good job." Now it should be, "Get a good education, then create a job."

COMING TO AMERICA—
THE LABOR HISTORY OF AFRICAN-AMERICANS

Most cultures that come to the United States arrive as immigrants. Many have landed on Ellis Island at the Statue of Liberty in New York City seeking religious, economic, or political freedom. They come to America with their cultures intact, believing that America is the land of unlimited opportunity. Such was not the case for the African-American. Instead of coming to America to be free, African-Americans were brought here to be a part of an economic system called slavery. Africans were pursued, purchased, and enslaved solely for the cheap labor they could provide on farms and plantations. Although their exact numbers will never be known, the estimates range from 3.5 million to more than 50 million Africans who were forcibly taken from Africa, and for every African who survived the rigors of transport to the New World, about five others died.[2]

There are some who rationalize slavery because so many of the slaves were introduced to Christianity. Quite a few of the slave owners sought to "Christianize the heathens" and bring them into "the fold." As a born-again believer, I appreciate the fact that many of the slave owners introduced us to the Bible and let us "have church." However, the real purpose of slavery was not a moral issue but an economic one. All of the Christianity issues were always subordinate to the slave owner's economic gain.

So the very reason Blacks are here in America has an economic foundation. The slave's sole purpose was to work to produce comfort and wealth for his master. I believe that our three-hundred-year history as slaves has affected the way we think about business and work today. Many Blacks are still too dependent upon the government and labor-related jobs, especially in inner cities. There are some that still believe that their situation is determined by what Whites do or fail to do for them. If we want a workable remedy to empower Black families to leave poverty, we must embrace God's Word, self-sufficiency, economic independence, and entrepreneurship. There are more Black people that work for the government than any other culture. We also seem to take more pride in defining whom we work for than working for ourselves. For instance, the business ownership ratio per thousand is 107 Lebanese, 93 Syrians, 89 Koreans, 65 Japanese, 64 White, 60 Chinese, 30 Columbians, 21 Jamaicans, 17 Hispanics, and 9 for African-Americans.[3] We need to do better than that.

Also, there are many who've asked the question, "Why aren't Blacks more self-sufficient like the Jews, Italians, or other ethnic groups?" I've often asked that same question. In January 2001, Jawanza Kunjufu of African-American Images in Chicago, IL spoke at Oak Cliff Bible Fellowship in Dallas, and he answered that question for me. He stated that comparing immigrants to slaves is not a fair comparison. Immigrants come to America with their cultures intact and also with a strong self-esteem, which can lead to a strong entrepreneurial spirit. The slave's self-esteem, on the other hand, had been broken and reduced, and for a long period of time he was legally denied the opportunity to be an employer, or an employee, but was required to be a slave.

Now don't get me wrong. Neither Kunjufu nor I am making up excuses for where we are today as a culture. However, I do believe that the myriad financial and business issues that African-Americans struggle with today are a result of our past experiences, beginning with slavery. No other racial or ethnic group has been confronted with such systematic opposition to their personal freedom, economic independence, and right to earn a living than Blacks have. That's why strongholds need to be broken, and attitudes need to be changed if we are to carry on a godly legacy of self-help and enterprise.

That's why it is imperative for Christians, especially African-Americans, to have God's perspective regarding work. In a typical week, most of us will spend more time at work than anywhere else. Actually, half of our lives are spent working. As far as the Lord is concerned, He is just as interested in what happens in our lives from nine to five during our workweek as He is on Sunday morning. Let's see what the Word of God says about the area of work.

GOD'S PERSPECTIVE ON WORK

God's way out of poverty and into financial health is through work. Productivity is the name of the game in God's kingdom. Even before the Fall, the time in which sin entered the human race, God started work. "The Lord God took the man and put him into the Garden of Eden to cultivate it and keep it" (Genesis 2:15). The very first thing the Lord did with the perfect man, Adam, in the perfect environment, Eden, was to give him a perfect job. Adam's first charge was to be productive! Despite what many have come to think, work was begun for our benefit in the sinless environment of the Garden of Eden. Work is not a result of the Curse. After the Fall, work was made more difficult. "Cursed is the ground because of you; in toil you shall eat of it all the days of your life. Both thorns and thistles it shall grow for you; and you shall eat the plants of the field; by the sweat of your face you shall eat bread" (Genesis 3:17–19).

The necessity of work

Work is so important that in Exodus 34:21 God commands, "You shall work six days." In the New Testament we discover that Paul is just as direct. "If any one will not work, neither let him eat" (2 Thessalonians 3:10 AMP). Examine this verse carefully. It says, "If any one will not work." It did not say, "If any one cannot work." This principle does not apply to those who are physically or mentally unable to work. It is for those who are able but choose not to work.

The problem with much of our contemporary welfare system is that it is an incentive not to work. Welfare as we know it today first appeared in the form of the Social Security Act of 1935. Government stepped in with new programs designed to get the country back on its feet. Part of the idea was to provide a safety net for the most unfortunate. The need was real. The intent was good. But the long-term side effects were bad for our sense of personal responsibility. Government gave us a crutch we've been leaning on more and more heavily ever since. That's what makes welfare wrong. I don't believe the concept of welfare is wrong but rather the way it has been used. For many recipients, it has been detrimental to their character. For instance, in order for some to qualify for welfare benefits, they must not be married and cannot work. Well, marriage and work are two things that God cares deeply about. In the African-American community, the growing welfare state has replaced the role of the father as breadwinner, while it has subsidized single mothers—including some who are still in their teens. Subsidize anything, and you're likely to get more of it. It's interesting to note that the rise of single parenthood and unemployment in our community has moved in tandem with increased welfare benefits.

One of the primary purposes of work is to develop character. While the carpenter is building a house, the house is also building the carpenter. His skill, diligence, and judgment are refined. A job is not merely a task designed to earn money; it's also intended to produce godly character in the life of the worker.

Dignity in all work

There's a story often told about the job attitudes of three bricklayers. When asked, "What are you doing?" the first bricklayer replied, "Laying brick." The second answered, "Making $9.30 an hour." And the third said, "Me, I'm building the world's greatest cathedral."

Now the story doesn't tell us what happened to these bricklayers in later years, but what do you think happened? Chances are that the first two bricklayers remained just that: bricklayers. They lacked vision. They lacked job respect. They lacked dignity. But I bet you the bricklayer that visualized himself building a great cathedral did not remain a bricklayer. Perhaps he became a foreman or a contractor or possibly an architect. I guarantee you he moved forward and upward. Why? Because the way a person works tells a lot about the person and his potential for larger responsibility.

According to Scripture, there is dignity in all types of work. Scripture does not elevate any honest profession above another. A wide variety of jobs is represented in the Bible. The Lord Jesus was a carpenter, David was a shepherd and a king, Luke was a doctor, Lydia was a retailer who sold purple fabric, Daniel was a government worker, Paul was a tent-maker, and Amos was a fig-picker. If God can use a fig-picker, He can certainly use us in our jobs!

In God's economy there is equal dignity in the labor of the auto-mobile mechanic and the president of General Motors, in the labor of the pastor and a secretary serving the church.

God's part in work

Scripture reveals three responsibilities the Lord has in work.

The Source of Job Skills
Exodus 36:1 illustrates this truth: "And every skillful person in whom the Lord has put skill and understanding to know how to perform all the work." God has given people a wide variety of abilities, manual skills, and intellectual capacities. It is not a matter of one person's being better than another; it is simply a matter of having received different abilities.

The Origin of Success
The life of Joseph is a perfect example of God's helping a person suc-ceed. "The Lord was with Joseph, so he became a successful man. . . . His master saw that the Lord was with him and how the Lord caused all that he did to prosper in his hand" (Genesis 39:2–3).

As we have seen, you and I have certain responsibilities, but we need to recognize that it is ultimately God who gives us success.

The Source of Promotion
Psalm 75:6–7 reads, "For promotion and power come from nowhere on earth, but only from God" (TLB). As much as it may surprise you, your boss is not the one who controls whether or not you will be promot-ed. Most people find this hard to believe. Our culture leaves God out of work. People believe they alone are responsible for their job skills and the control of their success and promotions. However, those with a biblical understanding will approach work with an entirely different mind-set. One of the major reasons people experience stress and frus-

tration in their jobs is because they don't understand God's part in work. Stop reading for a few minutes as you think about God's part: He gives you your skills and controls your success and promotions. This should give us tremendous hope in our work.

FIRST-CLASS CALLING, SECOND-CLASS TREATMENT

I am always amazed that some people think that preaching behind a pulpit is the ultimate ministry call. I've known quite a few businessmen who have quit their successful "secular" jobs to go into full-time ministry because they thought that was the only way they could significantly serve the kingdom. Now, I realize that many times God does call people to quit their jobs and go to work for a ministry. However, my concern is that too many Christians look at their jobs and careers as second-class callings, and many people in the church community make them feel that way.

After I committed my life to Christ and to the ministry, I was told by some well-meaning pastors that "when you really get saved, you'll quit all that business stuff and go into ministry full-time." At one point I became really confused because I never felt God wanted me to be a pastor. I would ask, "Why can't God use me in the business world too?" These men couldn't see why someone who was gifted in speaking and teaching would waste his gifts in the marketplace rather than be on the church's staff full-time.

I believe that God has given the vast majority of His people a ministry in the secular marketplace, and this is a calling that is just as important as being a pastor or missionary. You see, when it comes to our work, God does not distinguish between the sacred and the secular, and neither should we. If Christ is Lord over all of life, then He must be Lord over our work too. Think about some of the great men of faith in the Bible such as Abraham and Job. They were businessmen that God used mightily. Unfortunately, there is a mind-set out there that recognizes "church service" as the only viable ministry. However, in the kingdom of God, ministry is related to all the jurisdictions of life. If you are a lawyer, people ought to see how Jesus would try a case, through you. If you are a doctor, people ought to see how Jesus would treat the sick, through you. If you are a policeman, people ought to see how Jesus would enforce the law, through you. No matter what you do every day, you represent Jesus Christ in the workplace.

Ephesians 2:10 reads, "For we are His workmanship, created in Christ Jesus for good works, which God prepared beforehand so that we would walk in them." The Lord created each of us for a particular job, and He gave us the proper skills, aptitudes, and desires to accomplish this work. This calling may be full-time Christian service or a secular job. Often people struggle with whether God wants them to continue in their work once they commit their lives to Christ. Many feel they have to be a minister in order to serve Christ. Nothing could be further from the truth. The key is for each person to determine God's call for his or her life.

The examples on the following page are a parallel in the marketplace to the Ephesians 4:8–16 and 1 Corinthians 12 ecclesiastic ministries.

WHO'S YOUR BOSS?

Scripture reveals we are actually serving the Lord in our work— not people.

> Whatever you do, do your work heartily, as for the Lord rather than for men; knowing that from the Lord you will receive the reward of the inheritance. It is the Lord Christ whom you serve. (Colossians 3:23–24)

This is so important to understand. Consider your attitude toward work. If you could see the person of Jesus Christ as your boss, would you try to be more faithful on your job? The most important question you need to answer every day as you begin your work is: "For whom do I work?" You work for Christ.

Position	Spiritual Calling
CEO	Apostolic functions
Personnel	Pastoral
Sales	Evangelistic
Strategic planning	Prophetic
Administration	Government & helps
Systems	Teachers

THE BEAUTY OF HARD WORK

One of my favorite Scriptures is "Whatever your hand finds to do, do it with all your might" (Ecclesiastes 9:10). In Scripture, hard work and diligence are encouraged while laziness is repeatedly condemned: "He also who is slack in his work is brother to him who destroys" (Proverbs 18:9). The apostle Paul's life was an example of hard work. "With labor and hardship we kept working night and day so that we would not be a burden to any of you . . . in order to offer ourselves as a model for you, so that you would follow our example" (2 Thessalonians 3:8–9).

History has many examples of ordinary people achieving great things even against great odds. Business leader A. F. Herndon began his life as a slave in 1859. He moved from laboring in the fields of his master's farm outside of Social Circle, Georgia, to owning a highly successful Atlanta barbershop. From there, he went on to establish the Atlanta Life Insurance Company.

The late Booker T. Washington, an African-American educator of the late nineteenth and early twentieth centuries, constantly lectured his students about having a strong work ethic. He promoted hard work as the means of escape from the web of debt and sharecropping. His hope was that many would be successfully self-employed and become owners of land and small businesses.

This same commitment to a strong work ethic applies to us today. Your work should be at such a level that people will never equate laziness with God. Nothing less than hard work and the pursuit of excellence pleases the Lord. We are not required to be "superworkers," people who never make mistakes. Rather, the Lord expects us to do the best we possibly can.

OVERWORK: A SIGN OF MISPLACED PRIORITIES

If you are a "workaholic" and work all the time, take precautions to guard against forsaking the other priorities of life.

Exodus 34:21 reads, "You shall work six days, but on the seventh day you shall rest; even during plowing time and harvest you shall rest." I believe this Old Testament principle of resting one day out of seven has application for us today.

Rest can become an issue of faith. The question is, is the Lord able to make our six days of work more productive than seven days? Yes! The Lord instituted this weekly rest for our physical, mental, and spiritual health.

RESPONSIBILITIES OF A GODLY EMPLOYEE

We can identify the six responsibilities of the godly employee by examining the well-known story of Daniel in the lions' den. In Daniel 6 we are told that Darius, the king of Babylon, appointed 120 men to administer the government and 3 men, one of whom was Daniel, to supervise these administrators. King Darius decided to promote Daniel to govern the entire kingdom. Daniel's fellow employees then looked for a way to remove him from his job. After this failed, they asked King Darius to make a law requiring everyone to worship only the king or die in the lions' den. Daniel was thrown to the lions after refusing to stop worshiping the living God. The Lord then rescued Daniel by sending His angel to shut the lions' mouths. The six characteristics of a godly employee are:

1. Absolute honesty

Scripture tells us that Daniel's fellow employees could find no dishonesty in him, and there was no "evidence of corruption" (Daniel 6:4) in his work. He was absolutely honest. We will study the importance of absolute honesty in chapter 9.

2. Faithfulness

We discover the second characteristic of the godly employee in Daniel 6:4: "He was faithful." The godly employee needs to establish the goal of being faithful and excellent in work, then to work hard to reach that goal.

3. Prayerfulness

The godly employee is a person of prayer.

> Now when Daniel knew that the document was signed [restricting worship to the king alone] . . . he continued kneeling on his knees three times a day, praying and giving thanks before his God, as he had been doing previously (Daniel 6:10).

Daniel's job was that of governing the most powerful country of his day. Few of us will ever be faced with Daniel's responsibilities and the demands upon his time. Yet he knew the importance of prayer. If you are not praying consistently, your work is suffering.

4. Honoring your employer

"Daniel spoke to the king, 'O king, live forever!'" (Daniel 6:21). What a great response from Daniel. The king, his employer, had been tricked into sentencing Daniel to the lions' den. Think how natural it would have been to say something like, "You big dummy! The God who sent His angel to shut the lions' mouths is going to punish you!" But Daniel's reaction was to honor his boss.

The godly employee always honors his superior. One way to honor your employer is to never participate in gossip behind your employer's back, even if he or she is not an ideal person.

5. Honoring fellow employees

People may damage your reputation in order to get a promotion. Some may even try to have you fired from your job. Daniel's fellow employees tried to kill him. Despite this, there is no evidence that Daniel did anything but honor his fellow employees. Never slander a fellow employee behind his or her back. "Do not slander a slave to his master, or he will curse you and you will be found guilty" (Proverbs 30:10). Remember, your boss does not control your promotion; the Lord Himself does. We can be content in our job by trying to be faithful, honoring superiors, and encouraging our fellow employees. Having done this, we can rest, knowing that Christ will promote us if and when He chooses.

6. Verbalizing your faith

King Darius would never have known about the living God if Daniel had not communicated his faith while at work. The king said, "Daniel, servant of the living God, has your God, whom you constantly serve, been able to deliver you from the lions?" (Daniel 6:20).

Darius would not have been as powerfully influenced by Daniel sharing his faith if he had not seen him fulfilling his responsibilities with honesty and faithfulness. Listen to the words of Darius: "I make a decree that in all the dominion of my kingdom men are to fear and tremble before the God of Daniel; for He is the living God and enduring forever, and His kingdom is one which will not be destroyed, and His dominion will be forever" (Daniel 6:26).

Daniel influenced his employer, one of the most powerful people in the world, to believe in the only true and living God. You have that same opportunity in your own God-given sphere of work. Let me say this another way. A job well done earns you the right to tell others at work about the reality of Christ. As we view our work from God's perspective, dissatisfaction will turn to contentment for a job well done, and drudgery will become excitement over the prospect of introducing others to the Savior.

FROM EMPLOYEES TO ENTREPRENEURS

I will never forget the day I told my mother that I was going to pursue a career as a stockbroker. One of the first things she asked me was, "What kind of salary does it pay?" When I told her there was no salary and that it was a 100 percent commission job, she looked at me like I had lost my mind! "Boy, you're gonna starve!" she said. She added, "You need to find something stable and more predictable, with a good salary." My mother, like many of my uncles, aunts, and cousins, was an educator. They were good employees who believed that having a steady paycheck, good benefits, set hours, and job security was what most people should strive for. Nothing is wrong with that, but I decided, at twenty-four years old that I didn't want to go that route—I wanted to be different. I decided that I wanted to be an entrepreneur. The reward was no ceiling on my income. The risk was, if I didn't produce, I didn't eat.

During my first few years in the investment business, I desperately wished I had followed my mother's advice. In 1987, just one year after I became a stockbroker, the stock market crashed. More than 30 percent of all registered stockbrokers got laid off. At the time I was struggling, not making any money, and was thinking that the proverbial ax was about to fall on my head too. But I decided to hang in there, and now, I'm so glad I did. Today, I produce close to a million dollars in revenue. More important, I truly love what I do. After many years of very long hours, I now have flexibility and freedoms that many people wish they had. None of this could have been accomplished if I had not stepped out on faith, believed in myself, worked hard, and trusted God. I believe that more people in the African-American culture need to look at the benefits and take the calculated risk of being an entrepreneur.

Ephesians 3:20 (NIV) says, "Now to him who is able to do immeasurably more than all we ask or imagine, according to his power that is at work within us." This verse is talking about spiritual power. God possesses abundant power that He wants to bestow on us, both spiritually and economically. But as awesome as God's power is, His power in our lives will only be as strong as our capacity to handle it. For example, the Atlantic Ocean is a vast ocean with a lot of power. If you go to the Atlantic Ocean with a bucket's worth of capacity, you'll only get a bucket's worth of power. If you go to that same ocean with a couple of barrels' worth of capacity, you'll get a couple of barrels' worth of power. But if you go to the Atlantic with a reservoir's worth of capacity, you'll get a reservoir's worth of power.

Too many of us in the church and the African-American community are going to God praying to be a millionaire, praying for financial abundance, praying for power, but we only have a bucket's worth of capacity! Since God owns it all, we know there are vast resources available for us, but not enough of us have enough capacity to receive it. I believe one of the biggest economic problems in the African-American culture is that we have too many buckets (nine-to-five jobs) rather than reservoirs (independently owned businesses or positions that will allow unlimited income).

Have you ever noticed that other cultures don't look for corporate America or the government to be their savior? They start businesses and then hire family members to work in those businesses. They even live together in the same house to save money so they can build a solid enterprise. However, in the Black culture, it is still more prestigious to be a corporate executive than it is to operate a corner grocery store or a dry cleaners.

One of the ways that Blacks can control their own destiny is to pass down a legacy of wealth through entrepreneurship. Jobs are nearly impossible to pass down to the next generation, but entrepreneurship allows the opportunity to pass greater wealth on to our children. African-Americans who own their own businesses have five times the net worth of those who earn their incomes through salaries.[4] But entrepreneurship is not for everyone. Many people build wealth through more traditional methods: earning a salary, spending less than they earn, and investing in securities and real estate. Just because you're not a business owner doesn't mean that you can't build and leave a significant financial legacy for your family. For the purposes of this book, though, I will concentrate more on entrepreneurship because it seems to be a forgotten legacy in our community. Moreover, the changing economy, downsizing, and technological advances are forcing many of us to consider the benefits and the risk that entrepreneurship offers.

What is an entrepreneur? Even though I've always had the desire to be an entrepreneur, I didn't learn how to spell the word until a few years ago! The word *entrepreneur* is derived from a French military term, which means "to take risk for strategic gain." Jeffrey A. Timmons, in his insightful book *The Entrepreneurial Mind*, offers us a complete definition. There he writes, "Entrepreneurship is the ability to create and build something from practically nothing. It is initiating, doing, achieving, and building an enterprise or organization, rather than just watching, analyzing, or describing one. It is the knack for sensing an opportunity where others see chaos, contradiction, and confusion. Finally, it is a willingness to take calculated risk, both personal and financial, and then do everything possible to get the odds in your favor."

In his cutting-edge book *Black Economics*, Jawanza Kunjufu lists some of the personality traits of an entrepreneur. Included below are some of his questions as well as some of my own that everyone should honestly ask himself before embarking on starting a business.

- Are you a self-starter?
- Are you a risk-taker?
- Are you a hard worker?
- Can you make sound decisions under pressure?
- Do you possess good organization skills?
- Do you have good communication skills?
- Are you willing to work long hours?
- Can you deal with a fluctuating income?
- Are you resilient?
- Do you have a healthy self-esteem?
- Can you handle money well?
- Do you know how to manage people?
- Can you attract a diverse customer base?

These are just a few of the traits of an entrepreneur. As you can see, just because you can make the best sweet potato pie or fried chicken doesn't mean you are cut out to own your own business.

OTHER WORK ISSUES

Partnerships

Scripture clearly discourages business partnerships with those who do not know Christ. Second Corinthians 6:14–17 reads, "Do not be bound together [unequally yoked] with unbelievers; for what partnership have righteousness and lawlessness, or what fellowship has light with darkness? Or what harmony has Christ with Belial, or what has a believer in common with an unbeliever? Or what agreement has the temple of God with idols? For we are the temple of the living God; just as God said, 'I will dwell in them and walk among them; and I will be their God, and they shall be My people. Therefore, come out from their midst and be separate,' says the Lord."

In my opinion, we should also be very careful before entering into a partnership even with another Christian. I would consider only a few people as potential partners. These are people I have known well for years. I have observed their commitment to the Lord, I know their strengths and weaknesses, and I have seen them handle money faithfully. Do not rush into a partnership! Prayerfully evaluate it.

Before forming a partnership, put your understandings into writing. "But we've been friends for years," you may say. That may be true, but if you really value your friendship, you will protect it from a misunderstanding by putting the details of the agreement down on paper. In this written document, provide a way to dissolve the partnership. If you are not able to agree in writing, do not become partners.

Wives working outside the home

A recent survey by the Whirlpool Foundation and the New York–based Families and Work Institute indicated that nearly half of all married women say they provide half or more of their family's income. Many women today see themselves as the "new providers" in the family—especially in the African-American culture.

There are many reasons that women work outside the home. Married women work to provide income for their families, to express their creativity, or because they enjoy their job. Widows and divorcees usually must work to provide for the basic needs of their families. In my opinion, during the children's early formative years, if possible, it is wise for the mother to be home with the children, unless the family finances depend upon her income.

Titus 2:4–5 reads, "Encourage the young women to love their husbands, to love their children, to be sensible, pure, workers at home." Proverbs 31:10–31 reads: "An excellent wife . . . does [her husband] good and not evil all the days of her life. She looks for wool and flax and works with her hands. . . . she brings her food from afar. She rises also while it is still night and gives food to her household. . . . She considers a field and buys it; from her earnings she plants a vineyard. . . . She stretches out her hands to the distaff, and her hands grasp the spindle. She extends her hand to the poor. . . . She makes coverings for herself; her clothing is fine linen and purple. Her husband is known in the gates, when he sits among the elders of the land. She makes linen garments and sells them, and supplies belts to the tradesmen. . . . She looks well to the ways of her household, and does not eat the bread of idleness."

Proverbs 31 paints a picture of the working wife living a balanced life with the thrust of her activity toward the home. I believe my wife, Martica, is a perfect example of a Proverbs 31 woman. For the first five years of our marriage, she worked in corporate America. By that time we had two kids, but the long hours, stress, and constant travel were cutting into our family time. The money was good, but it just wasn't worth it. Furthermore, my income had increased enough to take care of the household needs. After quitting her corporate job, Martica decided to start a business from the home. Over the years, her business has prospered, and she now earns more income as an entrepreneur than she did as an employee working in corporate America. She also works fewer hours. Now she has the time and energy to focus on the kids and our marriage. When she was working outside the home, that was always a struggle. Having Martica work from the home has certainly been the best of both worlds. But it took some planning on our part.

You know what's interesting? If finances did not have to be considered, a third of the women in the Family and Work Institute survey would work part-time, 20 percent would do volunteer work, 31 percent would take care of their families full-time, and just 15 percent would work full-time.

Simply put, some women are gifted as homemakers, and there is no more important task than raising godly children. However, other women must work to earn income, or they have the skill and desire to work outside the home, or start businesses in the home like Martica. Either way, it is a decision that the husband and wife should make prayerfully and with full agreement.

Retirement: Being free to serve, not put out to pasture

The dictionary defines retirement as "withdrawal from an occupation or business, to give up or retreat from an active life." Many people retire when they begin to receive retirement income and stop all labor to live a life filled with leisure. Scripture gives no examples of people retiring and gives only one direct reference to retirement, which is found in Numbers 8:24–26. The instruction there applied exclusively to the Levites who worked at the tabernacle. As long as one is physically and mentally able, there is no scriptural basis for a person's retiring and becoming unproductive. The concept of putting an older but able person "out to pasture" is unbiblical. Age is no obstacle in finishing the work the Lord has for you to accomplish. He will provide you with the necessary strength. For example, Moses was eighty years old when he began his forty-year adventure leading the children of Israel. Scripture does imply that the type or the intensity of work may change as we grow older, a shifting of the gears to a less demanding pace in order to become more of an "elder seated at the gate." During this season of life, we can use the experience and wisdom gained over a lifetime. If we have sufficient income to meet our needs apart from our job, we may choose to leave the job to invest more time in serving others in whatever way the Lord directs.

Chapter Six

~ഏ ഏ~

SPENDING YOUR
MONEY WISELY

$\mathcal{I}$t was a beautiful spring Saturday afternoon, and I was looking forward to spending some uninterrupted time with my family and a few close friends. We had the barbecue on the grill, the baked beans were ready, and the potato salad looked delicious. My guests and I were ready to throw down! The last thing on my mind was business and finances. When the phone rang and my wife said it was for me, I told her to tell whomever it was that I would call the person back later. My wife then told me that it was Carlton, one of our church members, and that he needed to talk with me immediately. As much as I hated to, I came to the phone to see what was up.

Carlton is a doctor. He had been in private practice for about a year and a student in one of my financial classes the year before. He had accumulated about $250,000 of debt from his undergraduate and medical school education. He also had another $27,000 of credit-card debt and had just bought a new house with a huge mortgage. He was calling me from a Mercedes Benz dealership and needed my quick advice about a new car he was considering purchasing. When he told me that the car he was considering buying cost $92,000, I couldn't believe it. I thought he had lost his mind!

After the initial shock, I asked him about his current debts and income. He said that very little had changed in the last year. Then I asked him why in the world he would want to buy a $90,000 car with all of the debts that he had along with the responsibilities of a new medical practice. That's when things got pretty interesting. He told me that he was already approved for the loan (it's easy to get credit if you're a doctor because banks feel secure about a doctor's future income) and that the car he was considering was his dream car. I told him that I understood, but I thought it would be wiser for him to look for a pre-owned Mercedes for half the price. He took offense to my advice and then he blasted me, "Look here, Brother Lee, I am a doctor. I've worked hard for the last twenty years to become a doctor, and I deserve to drive the very best. Furthermore, I need to have a certain image," he said. Then he went on and on about his credit approval and how he could afford the monthly payments on the car. I even suggested that he take twenty-four hours to think about it. But there was no talking him out of it. When I sensed that I couldn't change his mind, I told him to go ahead and do whatever he wanted. You know, the funny thing about that call is I believe he had his mind made up long before he even phoned me. He was just looking for me to validate his decision since I was a financial adviser and one of the associate ministers at the church.

Why do you think Carlton was so adamant about buying this new car? What made him act so irresponsibly? It seems it was a sense of entitlement. Because so many middle-class African-Americans are working long hours, they feel entitled to a reward. And they want that reward now, not when they are fifty years old. What took our parents twenty years to acquire, we want to have in two years. Carlton was no different. He was a young, sharp, African-American male, who made a good income but spent it as fast as it came in.

A year later he confided in me that buying that car was one of the biggest mistakes he had ever made. He admitted to his financial immaturity and his inordinate desire to want to impress people through his spending. He lamented over the fact that he wasted so much money on the car because of some of his own internal issues. Unfortunately, there are a lot of people out there who are just like Carlton.

SPENDING OUR FUTURE?

Most Americans love to spend money! This is especially true in the African-American community. Many of us feel that after so many years of being deprived and not being allowed to enjoy even the simplest material comforts, we should make up for it by living extravagantly.

Today's African-Americans have more financial choices and career paths than our ancestors could have ever dreamed. I'm afraid, though, that our response to this newfound income would be a disappointment to our ancestors. Many slaves as well as the civil rights demonstrators suffered brutal lives to bring us to where we are today. We need to prove to them that we are worthy of the sacrifice, the blood, sweat, and tears that they invested in us.

Far too many of us spend money to prove to the world that we have arrived. We try to impress people by wearing our money on our back or driving it rather than putting it in the bank. However, trying to buy recognition, self-esteem, and respectability with material possessions is a waste of our Lord's resources, and it often puts us deeply in debt with little money saved. Let's not waste our money on things of which our ancestors wouldn't be proud. It's time to make a serious shift in our paradigm regarding our consumer choices if we are going to change our financial lives and greatly empower the next generation.

A LAND OF MILK, HONEY, AND CONSUMER CREDIT

Imagine a country with a per-capita income slightly more than that of Western Europe and considerably higher than the per-capita income of Asia, Africa, and Latin America combined. Imagine further a country where half of its fifteen million households own an automobile, which is one-third more than the former Soviet states, and more cars than in Asia, Africa, and Latin America together. Furthermore, imagine a country where one out of sixteen households owns two cars, and one out of one hundred owns three or more.

In this land of prosperity, 52 percent of the households own their homes, and 80 percent of these homes are equipped with two television sets, which is twice the number of sets that can be found in France or Italy and four times as in Sweden. These families have more members earning college degrees than the total student enrollment in England, Italy, and most of Europe. Even among the poorest of the poor, the majority has air-conditioning, a microwave, and twice as much living space as the average Japanese and four times as much space as the average Russian.[1]

Where is this country? you might ask. Surely, you would love to live there. Does it really exist? Yes, it does! It's Black America and the Black consumer market. Each year thirty-five million Black Americans spend billions—$550 billion in 2000—on goods and services. From New York to California, nothing elicits as much interest on Wall Street as what Black America buys with its enormous wealth. But there are some concerns.

The Coalition of Black Investors has pointed out that while Blacks are nearly 13 percent of the population, we earn just 7 percent of the income and control only 3 percent of the nation's material wealth. Some attribute this to the spending choices of Blacks. With an estimated annual income of about $550 billion, Blacks spend just 1 percent of that on education and less than .25 percent on technology (compared, for instance, to spending more than 5 percent on automobiles). As a matter of fact, Charles Schwab & Company issued a report a few years ago that said African-Americans' number one expense after basic necessities is their car payment, followed by their children's education. The same percentage of Whites say their number one expense after necessities is investing.

We know that very few African-Americans are poor, but as a culture, we typically spend more than what we earn. The typical African-American family making $35,000 a year spends money at the level of a White family making $50,000.[2] So the good news is that Black folks are making money. The bad news is what we're doing with it. Traditionally, we have been long on spending and short on investing.

MOVING FROM A CONSUMER MENTALITY
TO A PRODUCER MENTALITY

Did you know that the African-American community's income would place it as the ninth wealthiest country in the world? Unfortunately, though, 93 percent of our income is spent outside our community. I have read about many studies that have traced the flow of dollars from different ethnic groups. One said that in the Asian community, a dollar circulates in Asian circles up to twenty-eight days before it is spent with outsiders. In the Jewish community it was nineteen days; in the White community, seventeen days; but in the African-American community, six hours!

It seems that other ethnic groups have learned how to benefit greatly from our consumptive nature. Foreigners come to America, set up shop in a Black community, and make a killing off us. I've noticed that in many of these establishments the service is poor, they are impolite, and the prices are exorbitant, but what do we do? We continue to spend our hard-earned money with them. Now don't get me wrong—I'm not mad at them. Business is about seeing a need and filling it. However, I am mad at us for letting other ethnic groups come into our communities and fill needs that we should be filling. Every major American enterprise, especially non-African-American companies, recognizes that the revenues generated by Blacks can be the difference between eking out existence and determining a profit. Simply put, we're making other people rich. With black consumers spending 93 percent of their income outside the community, other cultures are reaping the benefits of double incomes; almost 100 percent of their own, and about 90 percent of ours. Essentially, many black consumers have joined other cultures in boycotting black communities and businesses.

Major marketers know that Blacks spend nearly as much as they earn and that we are immensely loyal to name-brand goods.

Even though we are about 13 percent of the U.S. population, African-American consumers purchase 36 percent of hair conditioners; 22 percent of malt liquors and movie theater tickets; 26 percent of Cadillacs; 22 percent of rice; 20 percent of portable television sets; 31 percent of cosmetics; 35 percent of soft drinks; 38 percent of cigarettes; and 25 to 35 percent of barbecue sauce, baby formula, detergent, potato chips, salt, pasta, toothpaste, and household cleaners.[3]

I think it is time for us to move from being a consumer-driven culture to being a producer-driven culture. A consumer spends and experiences constant *outflows* of money. A producer creates wealth by establishing entities that produce *inflows* of money. We need to start creating vehicles that keep more money circulating in our community instead of taking it out. One way of doing this is to increase the number of African-American–owned businesses. Our present numbers are nine African-American businesses per one thousand. The White community has sixty-four businesses per one thousand.[4] Maybe one of the solutions to the unemployment problem in our community is to increase the number of purchases made with African-American businesses.

Let's assume for this exercise that each year the African-American community earns $500 billion. Of the total amount earned, on average the Black community spends only 6.6 percent or $33 billion a year in African-American–owned businesses.[5]

Consequently, the amount of dollars that run through our hands and into the hands of non-Black enterprises without even circulating through the community once is about $467 billion. Now, if the African-American consumer spent just one-fifth of his money (twenty cents of each dollar earned) in the Black community, that would be $100 billion a year, which would translate to an additional $67 billion going back into our community!

I realize that it is unrealistic to expect that the majority of our dollars will be spent with African-American businesses, after all, we don't own enough businesses nor do we offer enough quality products to meet the demand of the Black consumer. I also realize that some of that $67 million that comes back to our community would be used to cover business expenses and taxes. Furthermore, all employees working for African-American–owned businesses may not be African-American; thus additional funds would be diverted outside the community.

The above example is used to illustrate a point. Basically, there is a tremendous amount that Blacks can do on their own without any additional inflow from mainstream America. Unfortunately, we still suffer from the old slave mentality that we don't trust one another. Too many of us still believe that the White man's ice is colder than a Black man's ice and that goods and services sold by African-American merchants are inferior to those sold by Whites.

I know that dealing with our people can sometimes be a lot of work. All of us have an "I've been burned by a brother or sister" story. Some Blacks even go so far as to say that because they've been burned, they'll never do business with Black folks again. You see, that's the difference between Blacks and Whites. When Whites get burned, they learn their lesson and move on. When we get burned, we hold it against the entire Black race! You'll rarely hear a White person—or an Asian or Jewish person—saying that about their race.

I do realize that there are some Black businesses out there who take their own people for granted. I've had to deal with Black businesses that open late, close early, and allow employees to treat customers rudely and talk on the telephone while I'm standing at the counter, and many other unprofessional practices. However, most of my experiences in doing business with our own people have been extremely positive. That's because I look for people that are competent no matter what their ethnic background may be. Whenever I have experienced egregious unprofessionalism from an African-American business, I tell them about it and then give them a chance to rectify it. Most of the time that works, but sometimes I have to move on. I may move on to another African-American business or I may not.

My point is this: Don't penalize or boycott a Black business just because it is Black. I believe this is not just an ethnic issue but also a kingdom one. If you don't like yourself, your skin color, your heritage, or the side of the railroad tracks you were born on, then you will be unfair and prejudiced against people who happen to look like you. If you don't have a healthy view of yourself, then you obviously can't have a healthy view of God. This is just as much a spiritual issue as it is a cultural one.

We also need to be thinking about various ways to strengthen our financial foundation and our legacy. The Bible says that we should leave an inheritance to our children's children. Maybe we should consider passing up the new BMWs and instead learn ways to pool capital, generate entrepreneurship, and build resources for investing in Black communities so we can create a future for our children. The power of the African-American dollar should never be underestimated; rather, it should be leveraged as much as possible.

A PLAN FOR SPENDING

At the end of each month, many of us ask the following questions: What happened to the money that I was going to save? What happened to the money I was going to give? What happened to my money, period? Where did it all go? It has been said that money talks, and when it does, it usually says good-bye! If you don't direct your money and tell it where to go, it will find a way to leave you. I believe that one of the best ways to gain control of your money is by developing a spending plan, more commonly referred to as the budget. A budget is simply a plan for your spending. It allows you to direct your money so you can reach your financial goals.

This reminds me of the story of a bank that notified one of its depositors that his checks had bounced. The man replied to the bank in disbelief, "I must have more money left in my account. I still have six checks in my checkbook!" Like the surprised depositor, if you do not have a written budget, chances are that you are flying by the seat of your financial pants.

To make a budget really work, you need to have self-control. This is a spiritual issue because it requires discipline and control of your desires and impulses. King Solomon accurately described the person who lacks self-control: "He who has no rule over his own spirit is like a city that is broken down and without walls" (Proverbs 25:28 AMP).

In ancient days, a city without walls was subject to any intruders who passed by and was thus in a state of constant disarray. Without self-control, your finances will dictate your decisions, instead of your decisions dictating your finances. Things like department store sales, impulse spending, putting things on layaway that you don't need, and buying stuff you can't afford will consume all of your income and more if you don't have the discipline and the intestinal fortitude to say no. Part of the fruit of God's Spirit is self-control, which basically means managing yourself.

IS YOUR UPKEEP YOUR DOWNFALL?

It has been said that if your expenses exceed your income, then your upkeep will be your downfall. Studies have shown that most people live from paycheck to paycheck. The average American spends $1.20 for every one dollar earned. This is called "living above your means," and it happens when your expenses *exceed* your income. Far too many of us live at the highest level we can afford. We max out on our home mortgage; we max out on the type of car we drive. I have seen countless examples of this in our culture—people who charge their credit cards to the limit, write postdated checks, take out bill-consolidation loans, and rob Peter to pay Paul. In the 1960s, Dr. Martin Luther King Jr. said that Black folks buy what they want and then beg for what they need. I wonder what he would say about our spending habits today. Some of us are literally spending ourselves into the poorhouse, but it's time for us to stop this destructive behavior and begin to spend less than we earn.

Regardless of how much a person earns, he or she probably will have "too much month at the end of the money" unless a carefully planned and disciplined approach to spending is established and followed. As you know by now, it's not how much you make but how you manage what you make. Regardless of your income level, the key to your financial peace and abundance is spending less than you earn. This means that your expenses should always be *less* than your income. Using a budget will help you gain the control needed to do that.

HOW TO BUDGET AND SPEND WISELY

A budget is only useful if it is used. It should be a plan tailor-made for managing *your* finances, not someone else's. Some people prefer using a handwritten system, while others are more comfortable using a budget system on computer.

To set up your budget, follow these three steps:

Step One: Begin where you are today.

Developing a budget must begin with your current situation. For one month make notes of all expenditures. Determine precisely how much money is earned and spent on a monthly basis. Most people don't know what they are actually spending and earning. For this reason it is essential to keep a record of every dollar earned and spent for a month to get an accurate picture of your estimated budget. If your income is not the same each month (like the income of a commissioned salesperson), make a conservative estimate of your annual income and divide by twelve to establish a working figure for your monthly income.

Then determine which expenses do not occur each month. Examples are real estate taxes and vacations. Estimate how much you spend for these each year and divide that amount by twelve to determine your monthly cost. Armed with this information, you can accurately complete the Estimated Monthly Budget on the next page. Do not be discouraged. Almost every budget starts out with expenditures in excess of income. But there is hope.

Step Two: Bring your income in line with your spending.

To solve the problem of spending more than you earn, you must either increase your income or decrease your expenditures. It is that simple (I never said it was easy, though). Either earn more money, or spend less money. There are no other alternatives.

Increasing Your Income

I have recommended that many people get a part-time job if they desire to bring their expenses in line with their income. There are always two concerns I have when I make this recommendation: 1) the person's spending will increase as he sees the extra money come in; 2) the person may sacrifice quality time with his family, and his spiritual life may suffer by working the extra hours. You must agree ahead of time with your family to put the extra income toward balancing the budget and not upgrading your lifestyle. You also need to agree on the extra

Estimated Budget

MONTHLY INCOME

GROSS MONTHLY INCOME [ ]

Salary _____
Interest _____
Dividends _____
Other Income _____

LESS

1. **Tithe/Giving** [ ]
2. **Taxes (Fed., State, FICA)** [ ]

NET SPENDABLE INCOME [ ]

MONTHLY LIVING EXPENSES

3. **Housing** [ ]
   Mortgage/Rent _____
   Insurance _____
   Property Taxes _____
   Electricity _____
   Gas _____
   Water _____
   Sanitation _____
   Telephone _____
   Maintenance _____
   Cable TV _____
   Other _____

4. **Food** [ ]

5. **Transportation** [ ]
   Payments _____
   Gas & Oil _____
   Insurance _____
   License/Taxes _____
   Maint./Repair/Replace _____
   Other _____

6. **Insurance** [ ]
   Life _____
   Health _____
   Other _____

7. **Debts** [ ]

8. **Entertainment/Recreation** [ ]
   Eating Out _____
   Baby-sitters _____
   Activities/Trips _____
   Vacation _____
   Pets _____
   Other _____

9. **Clothing** [ ]

10. **Savings** [ ]

11. **Medical Expenses** [ ]
    Doctor _____
    Dentist _____
    Prescriptions _____
    Other _____

12. **Miscellaneous** [ ]
    Toiletries/Cosmetics _____
    Beauty/Barber _____
    Laundry/Cleaning _____
    Allowances _____
    Subscriptions _____
    Gifts (incl. Christmas) _____
    Cash _____
    Other _____

13. **Investments** [ ]

14. **School/Child Care** [ ]
    Tuition _____
    Materials _____
    Transportation _____
    Day Care _____

TOTAL LIVING EXPENSES [ ]

INCOME VS. LIVING EXPENSES

NET SPENDABLE INCOME [ ]

LESS TOTAL LIVING EXPENSES [ ]

SURPLUS OR DEFICIT [ ]

days and hours you are willing to work so important relationships don't suffer.

Reducing Expenses

During the first five years of our marriage, Martica and I were riding high on our dual incomes. However, after we had our first two kids, we both decided that she would leave the corporate world to spend more time with the kids and start a business from the home. Her income at that time was about $50,000. As the day of resignation approached, I started to get nervous because I knew that $50,000 of our household income would be gone and that my income alone would have to take care of the family. This adjustment to one income taught me the habit of asking these questions about our expenses: Which are absolutely necessary? Which can we do without? Which can we reduce? You can ask these same questions of your personal budget as you work to reduce spending.

Some guidelines to help you evaluate your major expenses can be seen on the following page. Actual percentages may vary depending upon the cost of housing where you live, the size of your family, and your income. When you exceed the upper range in a category, this should warn you to carefully evaluate your spending in that category.

Consider these suggestions to spend money more wisely:

Shelter

1. Buy a modest-sized house suitable to your needs today with a design that can be expanded to meet your future needs. According to the IRS database, the average value of the American millionaire's home is estimated to be $277,000. Millionaires in the $2.5 to under $5 million net worth category live in homes worth $354,043, on average. Don't try to be the big shot by buying the biggest house on the block. You can't build wealth that way. Buy something you can afford. Preferably, purchase a home in the mid to low range of the neighborhood, and one that will appreciate in value.

Percentage Guideline

Category	Percent of Income
	(after giving and taxes)
Housing	25–38%
Food	10–15%
Transportation	10–15%
Insurance	3–7%
Debts	0–10%
Entertainment/Recreation	4–7%
Clothing	4–6%
Savings	5–10%
Medical/Dental	4–8%
Miscellaneous	4–8%
School/Child Care	5–10%
Investments	0–15%

2. Just because you live in an apartment doesn't necessarily mean that you are throwing money down the drain. Some people need to consider it. It is less expensive and involves fewer responsibilities—lawn care, maintenance, etc.
3. If you can do repair and maintenance work such as lawn care, pest control, painting, and carpet cleaning, you will save a substantial amount.

4. Lower the cost of utilities by limiting the use of heating, air-conditioning, lights, and appliances.
5. Shop carefully for furniture and appliances. Garage sales are a good source for reasonably priced household goods.
6. Married couples (especially men), please don't buy a house based on your and your wife's income. Try to base whether or not you can afford a house on the husband's income. There have been many wives I know that got pregnant, sick, or just wanted to quit working to devote more time to their children, but they couldn't because their mortgage payments required both incomes.

Food
1. Leave the children and hungry spouses at home when shopping. The fewer distractions, the better. And take a shopping list too.
2. Lunches and dinners eaten out are often budget breakers. A lunch prepared at home and taken to work will help the budget and the waistline. Consumer Credit Counseling studies revealed that more than 40 percent of a consumer's annual budget is spent in restaurants.
3. Shop once a week. Each time we go shopping for "some little thing," we always buy "some other little thing" as well.
4. Use coupons. It is unfortunate that the people with the least income use coupons less than those more financially stable.

Transportation
1. Purchase a low-cost used car and drive it until repairs become too expensive.
2. Avoid car leases unless you drive low miles and always want a car payment.
3. Perform routine maintenance—oil changes, lubrication, etc.— yourself. Regular maintenance will prolong the life of your car.
4. Do your research before buying a car. Find out the dealer cost, and don't pay the full markup for the car. Become a savvy negotiator.

Clothing

1. Shop in the off-season. Winter necessities, for instance, including coats, sweaters, and hats can typically be had at 40 percent to 60 percent off from January to March.
2. Don't be so name-brand conscious. Buy quality and what you can afford.
3. Avoid impulse purchases. Buy items that you had planned to buy. If some outfit really grabs you, take twenty-four hours and think about it. You will probably change your mind in twenty-four hours.

Insurance

1. Select insurance based on your needs and budget, and secure estimates from three major insurance companies.
2. Raising the deductible will substantially reduce premiums.
3. Seek the recommendation of friends or a skilled insurance agent. A capable agent can save you money.

Health

1. Practice preventative medicine. Your body will stay healthier when you get the proper amount of sleep, exercise, and nutrition.
2. Practice proper oral hygiene for healthier teeth and to reduce dental bills.
3. Ask friends to recommend competent physicians and dentists.

Entertainment and Recreation

1. Plan your vacation for the off-season and select destinations near home.
2. Rather than expensive entertainment, seek creative alternatives such as picnics or exploring free state parks.

Ten Budgeting and Spending Recommendations

1. Reconcile your checkbook each month.

At the end of each month, you need to sit down and balance your checkbook. The way to do this is to look at the previous month's bal-

TAKING CARE OF BUSINESS

ance and subtract all of the checks that you have written to come up
with your new monthly balance.

2. Have a separate savings account.

Use it to deposit the monthly allotment for those items that do not
come due each month. For example, if your annual insurance premium
is $960, deposit $80 in this savings account each month. This ensures the
money will be available when these payments come due.

3. Think yearly instead of monthly.

To better understand the impact of an expense, figure the yearly
cost. For example, if you spend six dollars for lunch each working day,
multiply six dollars by five days a week by fifty weeks a year. It totals
fifteen hundred dollars for lunches. Thinking yearly shows the true cost
of seemingly inconsequential expenses.

4. Control impulse spending.

Impulse spending ranges from buying big things like automobiles
to small things like tools. Each time you have the urge to spend for something not planned, pray about the purchase for several days. As you do
this, the impulse will often pass.

5. It is wise for husbands and wives to include personal allowances in their budget.

Both should be given allowances to spend as they please. This will
eliminate many arguments.

6. Examine your motives for making a purchase.

African-Americans often buy things to make us appear popular when
we really should select products that are more affordable. You should
never purchase an item to bolster poor self-esteem or because you want
to compete with someone else. Don't try to keep up with the Joneses.
Your purchases should be based on your own preferences and what
makes sense for you based on your income and lifestyle.

7. Don't buy extended warranties.

Most people never use them, so it's money that you're paying out for nothing. If you are still thinking about an extended warranty as added protection against costly repairs such as on a refrigerator or dishwasher, don't pay more than 10 percent of the product's price for the warranty.

8. Establish the difference between your needs and wants.

For the most part, any item that will impact your basic survival (health, food, and shelter) is probably something you need, and should take priority over anything you want. A want is an item that is not an absolute necessity. Cell phones and the type of car and clothes you wear are wants.

9. Don't be a conspicuous consumer.

Lavish spending on cars, clothes, and entertainment is one of our culture's most self-destructive habits. Many times a secondhand Honda Accord will do instead of a Lexus or Benz. Too many Black folks spend time trying to look wealthy instead of being wealthy.

10. Establish "finish lines" for your spending.

In other words, determine how much is enough, in advance. Too many Christians don't understand God's purpose for money. For most of us, the more we make, the more we spend. For the Christian, this is unacceptable. Every Christian should be able to determine how much money he needs to take care of his family and to carry out God's call on his life. Whatever amount you earn above that figure should not be spent, but rather used to fund God's kingdom and to help others. I know a man who decided that he would live off of $60,000 a year, and whatever he earned above that figure would go to the Lord's work. What about you? Do you have finish lines? What would you do if you had $2 million? Would you just raise your lifestyle to that level? Would you buy a Bentley? A couple of homes? How much would go to the kingdom of God? How much of the $2 million do you and your family really need? You need to be able to answer these questions if you are serious about being a good steward.

Step Three: How to find an extra $50 every month.

The most common temptation is to stop budgeting. Through the years there will be frustrations, but a budget, if properly used, will save thousands of dollars. Budgeting is kind of like staying in shape and exercising. Try to do it regularly, and you'll see enormous benefits. It will help you stay out of debt and accumulate savings. More important, it will help you control your life.

Where You Can Find an Extra $50 Each Month:
1. Brown bag ten lunches per month.
2. Make pizza at home instead of ordering out.
3. Use coupons for groceries, and buy store brands.
4. Avoid long-distance calls; stand while talking on the phone.
5. Rent movies and make popcorn at home instead of going out.
6. Get rid of your cell phone.
7. Give handmade cards and gifts.
8. Shop at consignment stores/thrift stores/discount outlets.
9. Request basic phone service only.
10. Eliminate cable television.

LEARNING TO BE CONTENT

The apostle Paul wrote in 1 Timothy 6:8: "If we have food and covering, with these we shall be content." Study this passage carefully. It says that if you have food and covering (clothes and shelter), you should be content. If this were an advertisement today, it would read something like this: "If you can afford the finest food to eat, wear the most expensive clothes and jewelry, drive the newest car, and live in a beautiful home, then you can be happy." Advertisers are experts at creating discontent so we will buy their products.

As a people, African-Americans are among the most discontented. Consequently, we are more influenced by the message that suggests that happiness, joy, and peace come to those who purchase the most stylish and prestigious things. Statistics show that we spend the most, save the least, and have the highest credit-card debt at almost every income level. Our discontent is rooted in our culture, which to a great extent is defined by conspicuous consumption and spending to impress others.

According to Howard Dayton, author of *Your Money Counts*, the word *contentment* is mentioned seven times in Scripture, and six times it has to do with money. Paul wrote, "I have learned to be content in whatever circumstances I am. I know how to get along with humble means, and I also know how to live in prosperity; in any and every circumstance I have learned the secret of being filled and going hungry, both of having abundance and suffering need. I can do all things through Him who strengthens me" (Philippians 4:11–13).

We are not born content; rather, we learn contentment. There are three elements to the secret of contentment: 1) knowing what God requires of a steward, that is, how to handle all the possessions that have been entrusted to you; 2) fulfilling those requirements faithfully; and 3) trusting God to do His part.

Note carefully that it is not just knowing these things that brings contentment; it is doing them. Once we have been faithful in the doing, we can be content in knowing that our heavenly Father will entrust the possessions He knows will be best for us at any particular time—whether much or little. Biblical contentment is an inner peace that accepts what God has chosen for our present vocation and financial situation. It doesn't mean that you don't strive for more or want to improve your life. It means that you are just content until you get there. Hebrews 13:5 emphasizes this: "Make sure that your character is free from the love of money, being content with what you have; for He Himself has said, 'I will never desert you, nor will I ever forsake you.'"

SEEK WISE COUNSEL

Many people have spending and money problems because they did not seek counsel before making decisions that have hurt them financially. People often avoid seeking advice because of pride or because they have already made up their minds to buy something, even if they cannot afford it. The Bible makes clear, however, that we need to seek counsel. Proverbs 19:20 (NIV) reads, "Listen to advice and accept instruction, and in the end you will be wise." Proverbs 12:15 says, "The way of a fool is right in his own eyes, but a wise man is he who listens to counsel." Before making a financial decision, you should subject it to three sources of counsel.

The counsel of Scripture

Psalm 119:24 (TLB)states, "Your laws are both my light and my counselors." Psalm 119:98–100 says, "Your commandments make me wiser than my enemies, for they are ever mine. I have more insight than all my teachers, for Your testimonies are my meditation. I understand more than the aged, because I have observed Your precepts." There are more than 2,350 Bible verses dealing with how we should handle money. If God's Word clearly answers my question, I don't need to seek any further. If the Bible is not specific about a particular issue, a second source of counsel is godly people.

The counsel of godly people (especially your wife, men)

The Christian life is not one of independence from other Christians but of dependence on one another. Each of us has a limited range of knowledge and experience. We need the insight and input of others who bring their own unique backgrounds to broaden our thinking with alternatives we would have never considered without their advice. The godly man is a good counselor because he is just and fair and knows right from wrong (Psalm 37:30–31). Seeking the counsel of your spouse, parent, mature Christian friend, mentor, or church leader is highly encouraged.

Now, to all the men, I'm not picking on you, but I have to say this: If you would just listen to your wife, and stop being so stubborn, maybe you would have the type of financial life you desire. Let all the women in the house say amen! My wife has saved me hundreds of thousands of dollars with her counsel and insight. I believe God has given women a special intuition and insight concerning their husbands. Men, that's why they are a helpmate to us, because we need their help! Most men, like myself, tend to focus on the facts and that's all that matters to us.

Throughout the years, as my wife met potential business partners of mine and heard me talk about doing certain business deals, she would sometimes say, "Lee, I just don't feel right about it." This used to drive me crazy! But I learned the hard way to listen to her counsel. As a matter of fact, I will not make a major decision regarding my business or personal life without my wife's input and agreement. Now I know some of you men may think I'm "henpecked" or that I don't "wear the pants" in my house. Hogwash! I believe that God gave me my wife to protect me and I'm not going to let my ego stand in the way of my blessings. I learned the hard way to listen to her counsel. Men, regardless of your wife's background or her financial aptitude, you must cultivate and seek her counsel. This will help preserve your relationship because you will both experience the consequences of a decision. If you both agree about a decision, even if it proves to be disastrous, your relationship is more likely to remain intact.

The counsel of the Lord

As we search the Bible and speak with godly people, we need to be seeking direction from the Lord through prayer. One of the Lord's names, according to Isaiah 9:6, is Wonderful Counselor. Often only the Lord can reveal to us the right direction, because only He knows the future. Listening for the counsel of the Lord is best accomplished in a quiet place with no distractions.

Counsel to avoid

Avoid the financial counsel of the wicked, those who live their lives without regard to God's values and principles. Foremost among these are fortune-tellers, palm readers, mediums, and spiritualists. This includes consulting horoscopes and all other practices of the occult. Never, *never* seek their direction.

POVERTY, PROSPERITY, OR STEWARDSHIP?

Many Christians embrace one of two extremes about finances. On the one hand, some believe that if you are really spiritual, you must be poor because wealth and a close relationship with Christ cannot coexist. On the other hand, others say that if a Christian is truly walking by faith, he will enjoy uninterrupted financial prosperity.

The Bible does not say that a godly person must live in poverty. A godly person may have material resources. Nor does it say that all Christians who truly have faith will always prosper. Study the life of Joseph. He is an example of a faithful person who experienced prosperity and poverty. He was born into a prosperous family, then was thrown into a pit and sold into slavery by his jealous brothers. While Joseph was a slave, his master, Potiphar, promoted him to be head of his household. Later he made the right decision not to commit adultery with Potiphar's wife. Yet, because of that decision, he was thrown in jail for years. In God's timing, he was ultimately elevated to the position of prime minister of Egypt. *The Scriptures do not teach that Christians must be poor.* A number of godly people in Scripture were among the wealthiest individuals of their day. *But neither does the Bible guarantee that we will be rich.* What the Bible does teach is the responsibility of being a faithful steward. Please review the diagram on the following page, which contrasts the three perspectives.

A LIFE WELL SPENT

As we have said before, our American culture and advertisers tell us to focus on today with no thought of tomorrow.

Let's examine two men who lived in Rome: One was rich, and one was poor.

In the Coliseum everyone would stand waiting for Caesar before the gladiator contests began. When Caesar arrived, he was greeted with shouts of "Hail, Caesar!" He had more power, fame, and money than anyone else living at that time. At that same time, there was another man in Rome in very different circumstances. He was in prison, investing his time praying and writing to friends. His name was Paul. One man

Prosperity, Poverty, Stewardship

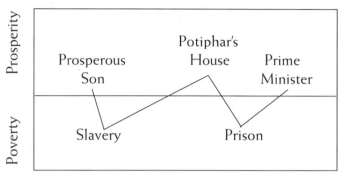

	Poverty	Stewardship	Prosperity
Possessions are:	Evil	A responsiblity	A right
I work to:	Meet only basic needs	Serve Christ	Become rich
Godly people are:	Poor	Faithful	Wealthy
Ungodly people are:	Wealthy	Unfaithful	Poor
I give:	Because I must	Because I love God	To get
My spending is:	Without gratitude to God	Prayerful and responsible	Carefree and and consumptive

lived in a palace; the other lived in prison. One was very rich; the other had almost nothing. One was the center of attention; the other was almost ignored. Almost two thousand years later, people around the world recognize which of these two men made the eternally important contribution. They name their children after the prisoner, Paul, and their salads after the emperor! Being used by Christ in a spiritually significant way has nothing to do with a high position or great riches. When you think about your spending, consider it in the light of eternity and being a faithful steward.

Chapter Seven

GIVING BACK
TO GOD

$\mathcal{O}$ne evening at church, I was teaching a class about the importance
of giving back to God. As I began to discuss the importance of tithes
and offerings, a guy named Wendell asked me, "Are you telling us that
we should give at least 10 percent of our money to God's work first,
before paying all of our bills? How would any of us survive if we did
that? How could we take care of our family's needs? What about all of
the debts that I have? Shouldn't I pay them off first?" Since we were
nearing the end of the class, I did not have the time to address all of
Wendell's questions. However, we did talk about his concerns after class,
and we looked up some Scripture verses that could answer his questions
on giving.

Wendell had grown up in a very traditional Black Baptist church that
hardly ever talked about tithing. He said he was accustomed to paying
dues, or participating in car washes, bake sales, fish fries, and bingo games
to raise money for the church. As a child, he gave quarters. Then as a
teenager, he would put a dollar or two in the offering plate. Now as an

adult, he proudly gave $20 to $50 a month to his church. Although he earned about $40,000 in yearly income, he erroneously thought he was tithing. He thought that tithing pertained to all Christian giving, and he didn't think the amount we actually gave to God was all that important.

I told him that the amount was very important to God, but our attitude was even more important. I explained to Wendell the difference between tithes and offerings and the benefits of giving to God first. I even shared with him some of my initial struggles with tithing. What I said really seemed to encourage him. He said, "Lee, I can see how God has blessed your life financially, and I can also see that this issue is clear in Scripture. Man, I'm going to go ahead and try God in this area."

In the coming weeks and months, Wendell told me story after story about how God was actively working in his family's finances. Wendell told me a few weeks later, "Man, I'm living better off 90 percent of my income than I've ever lived off 100 percent of my income." Even when trials came and his wife was laid off from her job, they were still fired up about their decision to honor God with their money. By making a spiritual decision to give to God first, Wendell and his family learned more about the love, care, and reality of Christ than any other time in their lives.

What about you? Have you tried God in this area? Do you understand the importance of your obedience in this area and the impact of giving in your life?

CAN'T BEAT GOD'S GIVING, NO MATTER HOW YOU TRY

As a child, I loved to hear the choir sing an offertory song entitled "You Can't Beat God's Giving, No Matter How You Try." I didn't understand what this song meant until I got older. But now as an adult who is committed to giving God's way, my testimony, as well as the testimony of many of my friends, is similar to the following story.

There was a farmer that was known for his generous giving, but his friends could not understand how he could give so much away and yet remain so prosperous. One day, one of his friends said, "We cannot understand you. You give far more than the rest of us, and yet you always seem to have more to give."

"Oh, that's easy to explain," the farmer said. "I keep shoveling into God's bin, and God keeps shoveling into mine, but God has a bigger shovel!"

The reason we can't beat God's giving is because none of us can out-give God. He has a bigger shovel, and He won't let us out-give Him. God will not be indebted to any man.

THE ATTITUDE IS MORE
IMPORTANT THAN THE AMOUNT

God's attitude about giving is best summed up in the very first Bible verse I memorized as a child, John 3:16: "For God so loved the world, that He gave His only begotten Son." Note that God gave because He loved. By sending His Son to die on the cross for us, He set the example of giving motivated by love.

In God's economy, our attitude is more important than the amount. The Pharisees would calculate the tithe right down to the last mint leaf in their gardens. God, however, looks past the amount of the gift to the heart of the giver. Christ rebuked them for their wrong attitude, saying: "Woe to you, scribes and Pharisees, hypocrites! For you tithe mint and dill and cummin, and have neglected the weightier provisions of the law: justice and mercy and faithfulness; but these are the things you should have done without neglecting the others" (Matthew 23:23).

For giving to be of any value, it must be done from a heart of love. When I give to my wife and children, it's not out of duty but out of my love for them. Stop and examine yourself. What is your attitude toward giving? Many people I know say they don't give because they don't want to make the preacher rich. What a lame excuse. Remember, when you give, your heart has to be right.

In addition to giving out of a heart filled with love, we are to give cheerfully. "Each one must do just as he has purposed in his heart, not grudgingly or under compulsion, for God loves a cheerful giver" (2 Corinthians 9:7). The original Greek word translated here as "cheerful" is *hilaros*, from which we get the English word *hilarious*. We are to be hilarious givers over the prospect of giving to Christ Himself.

There is usually little hilarity in the pews when the offering plate is passed at church. In fact, the atmosphere more often reminds me of a patient waiting in the dentist's chair, knowing a painful extraction is about to occur. How do we develop this hilarity in our giving? Consider the early churches of Macedonia.

"Now, brethren, we wish to make known to you the grace of God which has been given in the churches of Macedonia, that in a great ordeal of affliction their abundance of joy and their deep poverty overflowed in the wealth of their liberality" (2 Corinthians 8:1–2).

How did the Macedonians, who were in terrible circumstances, with "great . . . affliction and deep poverty," still manage to give with an "abundance of joy"? The answer is found in verse 5: "They first gave themselves to the Lord and to us by the will of God." Cheerful giving begins by submitting yourself to Christ. Ask Him to direct how much He wants you to give. Only by giving with the proper attitude are we put into a position to reap any of the advantages.

FOUR REASONS WHY
CHRISTIANS SHOULD GIVE

It is easy to understand how a gift helps the recipient. The local church continues its ministry, the hungry are fed, and the naked are clothed. But according to God's economy, a gift given with the proper attitude benefits the giver more than the receiver. "Remember the words of the Lord Jesus, that He Himself said, 'It is more blessed to give than to receive'" (Acts 20:35). As we examine Scripture, we find that the giver benefits in four significant areas:

Giving keeps our hearts turned toward God.

Above all else, giving directs our attention, affection, and hearts to Christ. Matthew 6:21 tells us, "For where your treasure is, there your heart will be also." In other words, wherever your money goes, that's where your heart will be. If I find out where your money is, I can then see what you truly value. That's why Rev. Billy Graham said, "A checkbook is a theological document; it tells you who and what you worship."

I know a lot of people who never cared about the stock market until they invested their hard-earned money. Now that they have invested in stocks, they look at the business pages every day, call me for updates, and closely monitor what happens in the financial markets. The stock market has their attention now because their treasure is invested there.

This is why it is so necessary to give each gift to the person of Jesus Christ. When the offering plate is being passed at church, we must remind ourselves that we're giving to the Lord. When you give your gift to Him, your heart will automatically be drawn to the Lord. Conversely, if you don't give your money to God, your relationship with Him will not be as intimate.

Giving breaks the power of selfishness.

Our heavenly Father wants His children to be conformed to the image of His Son. While humans are selfish by nature, the character of Christ is that of an unselfish giver. By regularly giving, we are continually being conformed to Christ. Someone once said, "Giving is not God's way of raising money; it is God's way of raising people into the likeness of His Son." The Lord understands that for us to develop into the people He wants us to be, we must learn how to share our possessions freely. If we don't, our inbred selfishness will grow and dominate us.

An extreme example is Howard Hughes. In his youth, Hughes was a typical playboy with a passion for parties and beautiful women and an aversion toward giving. As he grew older and turned an inheritance into a vast fortune, he became more and more closefisted. He let his wealth create an ever-increasing barrier between himself and other people. In his last years, he lived in seclusion and became a recluse whose life was devoted to avoiding germs and people.[1]

William Colgate is a sharp contrast to Howard Hughes. As a boy, he gave ten cents out of every dollar he earned to the Lord's work. As his business prospered, he increased his giving—first to two-tenths and finally reaching five-tenths. Then when his children were educated, he gave all his income to God.[2] God has also placed a prospering hand on men like H. J. Heinz of "57 Varieties" fame, H. P. Crowell of Quaker Oats, J. L. Kraft of Kraft Foods, and many others.

Simply put, giving helps us to break the power of stinginess in our life. It requires sacrifice and unselfishness to give.

Giving increases our heavenly account.

The Lord tells us that there really is something like the "First National Bank of Heaven," and He wants us to know that we can invest for eternity. "But store up for yourselves treasures in heaven, where neither moth nor rust destroys, and where thieves do not break in or steal" (Matthew 6:20). Paul also wrote, "Not that I seek the gift itself, but I seek for the profit which increases to your account" (Philippians 4:17).

As Christians, we can all transmute our money. The word "transmute" means to transfer something of a lower value to a higher value. For instance, you can transmute money into real estate. Whenever you invest $100,000 in real estate, it is your hope that the real estate will eventually become more valuable than the $100,000 that was originally invested. You want the lower value (the $100,000) to be transferred or transmuted into something with a higher value (the growth potential of real estate).

As base a thing as money is, it can be transmuted into an everlasting treasure. It can be converted into food for the hungry and clothing for the poor. It can keep a missionary actively winning lost souls. Any temporal possession can be turned into everlasting wealth, because whatever is given to Christ is immediately touched with immortality.[3]

And while it is true that we "can't take it with us," Scripture teaches that we can make deposits to our heavenly account before we die.

Giving increases our material blessings.

Many people give just to get, as if they are playing the lottery. Other people have a hard time believing that giving actually results in material blessings that flow back to the giver. Both of these paradigms are incorrect. To properly understand God's approach to giving, you must first understand the law of sowing and reaping. Simply stated, this law means, "Whatever we sow is what we will reap."

Consider the following passages.

There is one who scatters, yet increases all the more, and there is one who withholds what is justly due, but it results only in want. The generous man will be prosperous, and he who waters will himself be watered. (Proverbs 11:24–25)

Now this I say, he who sows sparingly will also reap sparingly, and he who sows bountifully will also reap bountifully. . . . And God is able to make all grace abound to you, so that always having all sufficiency in everything, you may have an abundance for every good deed; as it is written, "He scattered abroad, He gave to the poor, His righteousness endures forever." Now He who supplies seed to the sower and bread for food will supply and multiply your seed for sowing and increase the harvest of your righteousness; you will be enriched in everything for all liberality. (2 Corinthians 9:6, 8–11)

These verses clearly teach that giving does result in a material increase. Those who give "will also reap bountifully . . . always having all sufficiency in everything . . . may have an abundance . . . will supply and multiply your seed . . . will be enriched in everything." But note carefully why the Lord is returning an increase materially: "Always having all sufficiency in everything, you may have an abundance for every good deed . . . will supply and multiply your seed for sowing . . . you will be enriched in everything for all liberality." The Lord produces a material increase so that we may give more and have our needs met at the same time.

Giving → Needs Met → Material Increase → (Giving)

GIVING WHAT'S RIGHT, NOT WHAT'S LEFT

There's a story I heard a few years ago about a man who had two cows, one brown and one white. He decided that he was going to give one of them to the Lord but did not say which one. A few days later, one of the cows was attacked and eaten by wolves. The man then shook his head sadly and said, "Lord, it's a shame that Your cow died." This attitude of keeping the best and giving God the leftovers is pervasive in the church. As men and women of the kingdom, we should want to give God our first and our best because we recognize that all that is good comes from Him.

In Proverbs 3:9–10, Scripture exhorts us to honor the Lord with the first of our possessions. The Israelites gave God the "firstfruits," the firstborn of the flocks and the first crops gathered at harvesttime. For them, giving God the first and the best of their harvest indicated a recognition that everything belonged to Him.

Likewise, those of us who love the Lord should desire to give the first and best part of our income to the Lord. God deserves the best we have. Have you noticed that the government takes theirs right off the top? They don't even wait for you to decide. They don't trust you. Far too many of us get our paychecks (after taxes), then we pay our bills, and if there is enough left over, we give to God. That's not honoring God. The first check you write should be to God. This also cuts down on the temptation to rob God, as we will talk about next.

THE PRINCIPLE OF TITHING

Probably one of the toughest issues I had to deal with early in my walk with Christ was the issue of tithing. I was pretty much like Wendell in that I erroneously believed that tithing was representative of all giving in general. However, the meaning of the word "tithe" is "a tenth part." Today some people refer to it as tithing when they give $100 a month even though they make $2,000 a month. A tithe off of a $2,000 monthly income would be $200 (10 percent of one's gross income), not $100.

Now I know what some of you are thinking. *Did he say 10 percent of the gross amount? Man, you just ruined my day!* Yes, I said the gross, not the net. Remember, the quality of what we give to God is just as important as the quantity or amount. In Malachi 1:6–9, the Lord rebukes the Israelites because they offered defective animals as a sacrifice to the Lord instead of the very best that they had. The act was so insulting to God that He told them that their own government wouldn't be pleased with that kind of offering, let alone God. In other words, if the government doesn't accept anything but the best (a percentage of the gross), then why should God? In my opinion, giving a tithe after you have paid your taxes and other deductions means that you're not giving God your absolute best. You're also not giving Him the first. In the Old Testament, the Israelites were committed to giving God 10 percent because to do anything less was to "rob God." They believed that of whatever God provided them in the form of materials or cash or benefits of any sort, 10 percent belonged to God. It came off the top.

Before I talk about the importance of tithing for today's believer, let's look at one of the most important, yet misunderstood, passages in the Bible concerning tithes and offerings. Malachi 3:7–10 says,

> "From the days of your fathers you have turned aside from My statutes and have not kept them. Return to Me, and I will return to you," says the Lord of hosts. "But you say, 'How shall we return?' Will a man rob God? Yet you are robbing Me! But you say, 'How have we robbed You?' In tithes and offerings. You are cursed with a curse, for you are robbing Me, the whole nation of you! Bring the whole tithe into the storehouse, so that there may be food in My house, and test Me now in this," says the Lord of hosts, "if I will not open for you the windows of heaven and pour out for you a blessing until it overflows."

In this passage, God calls the Israelites thieves because they failed to honor Him with their tithes and offerings. As you know, a thief is someone who takes something that doesn't belong to him. In the Old Testament, the tithes belonged to God. However, the reason for the Israelites' theft was not financial but spiritual. The Israelites had actually left God. Although they were still in church, they weren't honoring God. Sounds familiar, doesn't it? When the question was asked, "How are we robbing You?" God needed to give the Israelites a tangible, physical illustration of their spiritual condition. God said, "Look at your finances. You're not tithing and giving offerings. The thermometer of your finances is saying that your spiritual temperature is cold!"

It's no different today. What we do with our money, especially in relation to giving, reflects where we are spiritually.

Now some of you may be saying, "Now Lee, isn't all that tithing stuff for the Old Testament?" Well, I'm glad you asked. Actually, the principle of the tithe pervades the entire Bible. You see, God has always asked mankind to give back to God a portion of what we receive from God. For example, Adam and Eve could eat from all the trees of the garden except one. That was a principle of the tithe, because in essence God was saying, "You can't touch this" (Genesis 2:16–17). The principle of the Sabbath is similar to the tithe (Genesis 2:2–3). Even before the Law, Abraham gave the first tithe recorded in the Bible (Genesis 14:17–20). Abraham did this as an expression of gratitude for God's deliverance in battle. Throughout Scripture, loving God and worshiping Him are at the heart of tithing.

THE GIVING OF OFFERINGS

Remember, however, that there were two robberies going on according to the prophet Malachi. One was of the tithes, the other of the offerings. One must understand that tithes and offerings were and still are completely different. The offerings were the gifts that were brought to God, over and above the tithes. You couldn't give offerings until you had tithed first. In other words, the offerings are what you give above the 10 percent. The Bible teaches that God demands the tithes, whereas He deserves our offerings. He demands the tithes because such giving is for our good and blessing. He deserves the offerings, for such overflow from our hearts satisfies His heart.

The best analogy I can think of for this distinction between tithes and offerings is when I first met my wife Martica. We actually met on a blind date. My sister and my mother met her a couple of months before I did, and they both thought that we would make a great couple. Well, I wasn't too excited about meeting her. However, I decided to follow through with meeting Martica out of a sense of duty to my sister and my mother. A funny thing happened, though. When I actually met Martica, I enjoyed her company so much that I decided that I wanted to take her out again, and again, and again. Needless to say, I took her right to the marriage altar! You see, the first time I saw Martica was out of obedience and duty to my mother and sister. However, the second time, third time, fourth time, etc., was of my own free will. The first time I had to take her out; the second time I wanted to take her out.

Similarly, Christians tithe because God demands it. We do it out of obedience. Tithing is a debt we owe, and it is mandatory. We give offerings because we are just so in love with God that we can't help ourselves. Offerings are a seed we sow, and they are given voluntarily.

The New Testament teaches that we are to give in proportion to the material blessings we have received. The New Testament also commends sacrificial giving. What I like about the tithe or any fixed percentage of giving is that the amount is easy to compute. On the other hand, the danger of tithing is that it can be treated as simply another bill to be paid. Remember that giving is a form of worship. Tithing with a wrong attitude will not put you in a position to receive the blessings God has for you. Another potential danger of tithing is the assumption that once the tithe is given, all my obligations to give to the kingdom are fulfilled. For many Christians, the tithe should be the beginning of their giving, not the limit. In my family, we are convinced that we should tithe as a minimum and then give over and above the tithe as the Lord prospers or directs us.

COMMON EXCUSES FOR NOT GIVING

As I go around the country speaking on the subject of stewardship, I am amazed at some of the excuses I hear from people regarding giving. Below I've listed just a few.

I can't afford to give.

You mean to tell me if your salary was reduced by 10 percent you wouldn't continue to live? Actually, you can't afford not to give—especially those of you who are in debt. I can't explain it except to say that when you honor God with your giving, something supernatural happens. Living off 90 percent of your income allows God to step in and make it go further than 100 percent. A lot of people say they can't afford to tithe, but their tithes are on their back and on their feet and in their garages. Many times the money is there to honor God, but we spend it in other places.

I don't trust the leaders with the money I give.

When you give money to your church, you are actually giving to the Lord. God will honor your obedience to Him regardless of what happens to the money once it leaves your hand. If a church leader goes and runs off with the entire offering, that doesn't nullify the blessings owed to you. All of us should want to plant our seed into good ground. Therefore, if you don't trust your leaders with money, and if you are worried about what happens to it once you give, then you need to check your own heart first. If your heart is right, then you need to find a leader you can trust so you can continue to honor God.

Ten percent is just too much.

How could 10 percent be too much? God allows us to keep 90 percent. Man, that's a great deal! The government doesn't even allow us to keep that much! I remember one day a lady came up to me after I spoke at her church and said that she had just received a large settlement, about $200,000, in fact. She asked me, "Lee, what should the tithe be off of that amount?" When I told her $20,000 she said, "Oh no, that's too much to give to God." I asked her if she tithed her present income, and she said, "Sometimes I do." You see, her problem was simple: She was never faithful with her small income, so when she received the settlement, she couldn't be faithful with a larger amount. If you are robbing God with the small amount you earn, which is petty theft, why should God bless you with more money so you can commit grand larceny?

I want to get out of debt first.

Why are you in debt in the first place? Is that God's fault? Is God responsible for unwise and greedy decisions? So you're telling me you would rather rob God to pay men? I believe even if you have come into the debt legitimately, your first debt is to God. If we honor God and make wise financial decisions, He will help us get out of debt and experience true financial freedom.

PLACES FOR GIVING

We are instructed in Scripture to give to three areas. To whom and in what proportion one gives varies with the needs God lays on the heart of each believer.

Giving to the local church and Christian ministries

Again in Malachi 3:10 it says, "Bring the whole tithe into the storehouse, so that there may be food in My house." In the Old Testament, there was a storehouse in the sanctuary, built for depositing the tithes and offerings of the people. The New Testament counterpart of this principle is that church members give all their tithes to the local church. "Storehouse tithing" means to bring your tithes to the church where your membership is established, your spiritual life is nourished, and your church privileges are enjoyed. If you give elsewhere, then it should be over and above the required tithe to your church.

"Why is that so?" you may ask. Again in the Old Testament, the priesthood was to receive support: "To the sons of Levi, behold, I have given all the tithe in Israel . . . in return for their service which they perform, the service of the tent of meeting" (Numbers 18:21). The New Testament teaching on ministerial support is just as strong. Unfortunately, some have wrongly taught that those who are in Christian ministry should be poor. That position is not scriptural. Pastors who do their work well should be paid well and should be highly appreciated, especially those who work hard at both preaching and teaching (1 Timothy 5:17–18).

God never intended for pastors to exist as paupers while those who are enriched by their ministry live as princes. On the other hand, God never intended for pastors to live like princes while those in the congregation live like paupers. I must admit I've seen abuses on both sides. I know pastors who think they need to stay broke and humble in order to serve the Lord. I also know some pastors who live so extravagantly that they are a stumbling block to the very people they are trying to reach.

In the Black church, the pastor is often expected to display the trappings of success even though most preachers make ordinary money. Some congregations even buy luxury cars for their pastors. Because African-Americans tend to esteem their pastors higher than other cultures do, we typically want them to look good because they represent the membership. There is absolutely nothing wrong with this way of thinking. In Galatians 6:6 it says, "The one who is taught the word is to share all good things with the one who teaches him." Most committed church members should want their pastors to live in nice homes and wear nice clothes, but a lot of preachers take that to the extreme. They don't want to live in a comfortable home; they want a mansion—with servants! Now, I'm all for pastors living very well, because in many cases they are leading multimillion-dollar enterprises. Being a pastor is hard work. However, with such power and authority comes accountability.

Unfortunately, the lack of financial accountability in many churches would be shocking to the business world. If businesses handled their financial affairs the way some churches do, they would be out of business. And if business leaders handled their company's finances the way some pastors handle their church's finances, they would get fired. It's time for the church to get its financial house in order, starting from the top down. With professional people in the pews, skeptical media, and government agencies scrutinizing church activities, churches must meet a higher standard of professionalism than in the past. They have to become more businesslike.

Giving to family members

In our culture, we are experiencing a tragic breakdown in this area of giving. Husbands have failed to provide for their wives, parents have neglected their children, and grown sons and daughters have forsaken their elderly parents. Such neglect is condemned. The Bible states that not taking care of one's family is tantamount to being an unbeliever.

Meeting the needs of your family and relatives is a priority in giving. What should you do about family members and friends who ask for financial loans? Some time ago my wife and I decided that when we help someone financially, it would be better for us to give him or her money rather than loan them money. One of the reasons we made this decision was because we didn't want people in bondage to us. The second reason was some of the people we loaned money to never repaid us. I don't have to tell you what that can do to a relationship. I'm not saying you should never loan money to relatives or friends, but if you can, try to give them the money instead. It will be more of a blessing to them and to you.

Giving to those in need

There are hundreds and hundreds of verses in the Bible that deal with giving to the needy. In Matthew 25, we are confronted with one of the most exciting and yet sobering truths in Scripture. Read this passage carefully:

> "Then the King will say . . . 'For I was hungry, and you gave Me something to eat; I was thirsty, and you gave Me something to drink. . . .' Then the righteous will answer Him, 'Lord, when did we see You hungry, and feed You, or thirsty, and give You something to drink?' . . . . The King will answer and say to them, 'Truly I say to you, to the extent that you did it to one of these brothers of Mine, even the least of them, you did it to Me.' Then He will also say to those on His left, 'Depart from Me, accursed ones, into the eternal fire; . . . for I was hungry, and you gave Me

nothing to eat; I was thirsty, and you gave Me nothing to drink. . . . Truly I say to you, to the extent that you did not do it to one of the least of these, you did not do it to Me.'" (Matthew 25:3, 37, 40–42, 45)

In some mysterious way that we cannot fully understand, Jesus, the Creator of all things, identifies Himself with those in need. When we share with them, we are actually sharing with Jesus Himself. And when we do not give to the needy, we leave Christ Himself hungry and thirsty.

During Christ's earthly ministry, He gave consistently to the needy. It is especially revealing that during the Last Supper, after Jesus told Judas to go and carry out the betrayal, this comment is made:

> Now no one of those reclining at the table knew for what purpose He had said this to him. For some were supposing, because Judas had the money box, that Jesus was saying to him, "Buy the things we have need of for the feast"; or else, that he should give something to the poor. (John 13:28–29)

Giving to the needy was such a consistent part of Jesus' life that the disciples assumed that Jesus was sending Judas either to buy food or to give to the poor—no other alternative entered their minds.

Giving or lack of giving to the needy affects three areas of our Christian life:

1. A lack of giving to the needy could be a source of unanswered prayer. "Is this not the fast which I choose . . . ? Is it not to divide your bread with the hungry and bring the homeless poor into the house . . . ? Then you will call, and the Lord will answer" (Isaiah 58:6–7, 9a). "He who shuts his ear to the cry of the poor will also cry himself and not be answered" (Proverbs 21:13).
2. Our provision is conditioned upon our giving to the needy. "He who gives to the poor will never want, but he who shuts his eyes will have many curses" (Proverbs 28:27).
3. One who does not share with those in need does not know the Lord intimately. "He pled the cause of the afflicted and the needy;

then it was well. 'Is not that what it means to know Me?' declares the Lord" (Jeremiah 22:16).

I believe that primarily it's the church's responsibility to help the needy. If people would give to God's work the way they are supposed to, we wouldn't need welfare at all. The church has the potential to do far more than the government could ever do.

I pray that you and I might be able to echo Job's statement: "I delivered the poor who cried for help, and the orphan who had no helper . . . and I made the widow's heart sing for joy. . . . I was eyes to the blind and feet to the lame. I was a father to the needy, and I investigated the case which I did not know" (Job 29:12–13, 15–16).

I want to encourage you to purpose in your heart that starting with your next paycheck, you will be a faithful, consistent giver. The most fulfilled people I have known are those who have been generous, not stingy.

Chapter Eight
PUTTING YOUR MONEY TO WORK

$\mathcal{A}$t the September 1995 annual Black Congressional Caucus dinner, the guest of honor was Osceola McCarthy, a quiet, unassuming
Black woman from Hattiesburg, Mississippi. As celebrities and politicians made many speeches about generosity, McCarthy sat humbly listening and seemed somewhat perplexed when she was given a standing
ovation as the one person who deserved the most recognition that
evening. At eighty-five, she had just created a $250,000 scholarship trust
at the University of Mississippi. She designated that the funds be used
for the education of poor students—not necessarily Black—who could
not afford a college education. McCarthy was not a wealthy business-
woman creating an endowment from inherited wealth. She was a laun-
drywoman who dropped out of school after completing only the sixth
grade. She amassed more than $250,000 over her lifetime by faithfully
saving the money she earned washing and ironing clothes for $1.50 to
$10 a bundle. McCarthy started saving nickels, dimes, and whatever
change she made from running errands. As she got older, she set aside

her money from doing laundry to cover her living expenses and put the rest—about $200 a month—into savings accounts. McCarthy, who never married or had children, epitomized "living beneath your means." For the seventy-five years that she worked, she never had a credit card, did not own a car, had no air-conditioning in her small house, and never possessed a television or a VCR. She followed the basic, simple principle of disciplined savings and consistent deposits into her account and held a sacred belief in the concept of compound interest.

SAVING, INVESTING, AND THE AFRICAN-AMERICAN

You're not saving enough! The message has been hammering away at Americans for years. Our savings rate, compared to other countries, has historically been low. Many Americans believe they stand a better chance of getting rich from lotteries or sweepstakes than from saving and investing. The average person in our country is three weeks away from bankruptcy. He has significant debt, little or no money saved, and is totally dependent on next week's paycheck to keep the budget afloat. Thirty-five percent of all adults in our country have no savings at all.[1]

In the African-American culture, the lack of saving and investing is even more pervasive. U.S. Census statistics in the mid-1990s confirm that the savings rate for all Americans is 3.9 percent, but African-Americans save less than half the national average—1.8 percent. Also, Blacks own less than 1 percent of the available stocks and bonds in the country, yet make up nearly 13 percent of the population.[2] For many Black families, saving and investing is a new concept, because historically many of our families were forced to live according to their immediate needs and not for the future. Financial planning was not an option for many of our ancestors; life was about financial survival. As a culture, we know how to work for money; now it's time for us to put our money to work!

THE JOSEPH PRINCIPLE

Scripture encourages us to save. "The wise man saves for the future, but the foolish man spends whatever he gets" (Proverbs 21:20 TLB). The ant is commended for saving for a future need. "Four things on earth are small, yet they are extremely wise: Ants are creatures of little strength, yet they store up their food in the summer" (Proverbs 30:24–25 NIV). Saving is the opposite of debt. Saving is making provision for tomorrow, while debt is presumption upon tomorrow.

I call saving the "Joseph principle," because saving requires self-denial. Joseph saved during the seven years of plenty to survive during the seven years of famine. Saving is denying expenditure today so that you will have something to spend in the future. One of the major reasons most people are poor savers is that we live in a culture of self-indulgence, not self-denial. When we want something, we want it now!

THE KEY TO SAVING MONEY
IS TO PAY YOURSELF SECOND

The most effective way to save is not to pay yourself first but to pay yourself second. When you get paid, the first check you write should be for giving to the Lord, and the second check for your savings. An automatic payroll deduction can be very helpful to ensure that a portion of your income is saved regularly. Some commit income from tax refunds or bonuses to be saved. Recognize this: If you immediately save a portion of your income each time you are paid, you will save more. The Bible does not teach a percentage to be saved. I recommend establishing a goal to save 10 percent of your income. For many this is not possible in the beginning. But begin the habit of saving, even if it's only ten dollars a month.

ESTABLISH LONG- AND SHORT-TERM SAVINGS

Long-term savings are intended to fund future needs and goals, such as retirement or the college education of your kids. Also, any stock and bond mutual funds as well as individual stocks should also fall in the long-term savings category. Except for financial emergencies, these savings should not be used for any other purpose. They could be called "never-to-spend savings."

Short-term savings should be in an account that is easily accessible. It may include interest-bearing accounts, money-market mutual funds, and so forth. These funds are designed to be used for planned future spending, such as a car or the down payment on a home. Short-term savings should also be set aside for emergencies—an illness, loss of job, or other interruption of income. I usually recommend that people establish the goal of saving two to three months of their income for this emergency fund.

THE SEVEN GREAT GOALS OF INVESTING

Before you decide how you are going to save and invest, you must first determine why you should invest. Deuteronomy 8:18 says that it is God who gives us the ability to become wealthy so that He may confirm His covenant. You see, God is not against your acquiring wealth, as long as you have a kingdom purpose. God is not against you taking risk either, or to use a more comfortable term, God is not against you investing.

In Matthew 25:14–30, Jesus tells the story of a man who left his money with three of his servants to take and invest. The master commended the first two servants who had invested wisely and doubled his money. I think they had to take risks to get that type of return.

The third servant buried his money and took no risk. He was scared, so he played it safe. The master condemned him, saying, "How dare you take what does not belong to you and not make more with it? The least you should have done was put it in the bank and make me some interest."

Did you know there are many Christians who are scared to take legitimate risk? They have never taken the time, talents, and treasures God has given them and maximized them. The Lord needs more legitimate risk-takers to build a snowball of wealth that can be used for the kingdom and passed from generation to generation. History has proven that investing is one of the best ways to accumulate wealth and, more important, to pass it on.

However, before we begin to invest, we must make sure we have the right motives. I believe that all legitimate and biblical investing should flow from what I call the Seven Great Goals of Investing. They are as follows:

1. To have a long, comfortable, worry-free retirement without any real concern about ever running out of money.

The ants in Proverbs 30:25 diligently prepare their food in the summer, because they know when the winter comes, they will not have the same opportunity to gather food. If you keep living, there will be a "winter season" in your life too. This winter season is called retirement. Investing for your retirement is a legitimate reason to invest, because one day you will get old, and you probably won't have the physical energy or the income opportunities that you have today. Think of retirement as the longest vacation you will ever take. However, the catch is that you have to pay for this vacation in advance.

Because of strides our society has made in health care, technology, and overall physical fitness, you can expect to live longer than members of past generations. Life expectancies in this country have climbed dramatically during this century. In 1920, the average life expectancy at birth was just more than 54 years. Retirement, when reached at all, generally lasted only a few years. However, by 1996, average life expectancy for people born in 1996 had risen to 76.1 years. According to the *New York Times* article printed on September 12, 1997, that's a twenty-two-year increase in this century alone! Tens of thousands of people are breaking the one-hundred-year mark, and it's not unrealistic to assume that you will live well into your eighties, perhaps even into your nineties. That's the good news. The bad news is that you may live so long that you outlive your assets and end up without adequate income during a time when you should be free of financial worries.

I know that some of you may say, "Brother Lee, I'm not worried about retirement, because the writer of Psalm 37 said that he had never seen the righteous forsaken or his seed begging for bread." Well, you are exactly right. God certainly does take care of His righteous servants, but we have a responsibility, too. Retirement planning is not about merely surviving; it's also about your quality of life.

Well, what do you need to do? Number one, you need to take charge of your own retirement planning and start today. Don't leave it to chance and don't rely solely on Social Security. The Social Security system was originally designed to serve as a safety net, not as a sole support in retirement. Number two, if your company has a 401(k) plan, make maximum contributions to this tax-deferred retirement vehicle. Also, look into an IRA, regardless of whether or not your contributions are tax deductible. Though the amounts you can put away are relatively small, the dollars can add up over time.

2. *To intervene in the financial lives of one's children.*

First Timothy 5:8 reads, "If anyone does not provide for his own, and especially for those of his household, he has denied the faith and is worse than an unbeliever." Also, in 2 Corinthians 12:14 it says that parents are responsible for saving money for their children. This principle extends to providing for your family's needs during your lifetime and/or in the form of legacies. There are three main financial reasons that my wife and I invest for our three children. One is to help them buy their first home, the other is to help them build a business that they may own, and third, to provide for their college education. As we do these things for our kids, we expect them to meet certain character, academic, and spiritual requirements that we set.

Let's take college for an example. Sending children to college is a classic "rock and a hard place" dilemma for many parents. On one side, you want your children to get as much education as possible. On the other, paying for that education can drive you tens of thousands of dollars into debt if you don't have a plan.

According to a 1997 College Board study, the average sticker price for a college education from a four-year public institution will run $30,000, or $7,500 a year. At private colleges, it can top $77,000. Some of us may shell out more money to educate our kids than we did to purchase our first house. I believe that it is worth it for parents to make this kind of investment, especially in African-American children. The difference in average lifetime earnings between a high school graduate and a college graduate can be more than a million dollars, which makes college a sound investment. Our children need to be able to compete at the highest levels possible. We need to start raising intellectual and spiritual giants that will make a difference in this world. It's going to take money to educate the next Dr. Martin Luther King Jr., Thurgood Marshall, or Colin Powell. Seek scholarships and financial aid and start stashing away money in a college fund as soon as you can. Also, make sure you have adequate life insurance so if something happens to you, your child can still be educated.

3. To intervene in the financial lives of one's grandchildren.

Proverbs 13:22 states that "a good man leaves an inheritance to his children's children." Remember, when God sees you, He sees three generations in you: you, your children, and your grandchildren. Therefore all of your financial planning and investing should have a multigenerational approach to it, because that's how God thinks. One of my business colleagues told me that he is able to invest an extra $35,000 a year in the stock market because his parents take care of the private school tuition for his three children. This is an expense that would have belonged to him, but instead he can save his money and continue to build his wealth. That's why generational thinking is so powerful. It helps the grandchildren, but it can also help the parents.

4. To care for one's parents if and when they need it.

Because people are living longer, many of us may become financially responsible for our parents at some point. With the aging of the seventy-six million baby boomers, this is becoming an increasingly important issue. Estimates suggest that almost one in five workers will be caring for an older adult. I have seen a few of my clients build great investment portfolios, only to watch those portfolios vaporize over the years because a client's mom had to go to a nursing home. This type of care can be very expensive. That's why long-term care insurance is important. This type of insurance covers some of the cost of services that may be rendered to an elderly parent. Services associated with everyday activities of living, such as eating, bathing, dressing, and getting out of bed or getting out of a chair, are covered under this plan. This type of care generally does not involve hospitals but can be provided in the home, in nursing homes, or in assisted-living facilities.

5. To leave an important legacy to a charity, church, or institution one believes in.

This issue is about your personal values more than financial planning. Many people feel it's important to buy their immortality. In other words, they give money to a particular place so the values and principles that they hold dear can be perpetuated. In this way, your money can continue to speak for you long after you are gone. As you grow your wealth through investing, consider leaving a substantial portion to your church or a beloved school or charity. Osceola McCarthy did this, and her legacy will be felt throughout many generations.

6. To become financially free to serve the Lord.

One objective for saving is to reduce our dependence upon a salary to meet our needs. With adequate investments, we may have the freedom to respond if the Lord leads us to invest more volunteer time in ministry. The more income my savings produce, the less I am dependent upon my salary. Some have saved enough to be free one day a week, and others are in a position to be full-time volunteers without the need to earn a salary. I know a couple that sensed the Lord wanted them to save steadily so that by age fifty-five they would be free to volunteer full-time serving a ministry. This couple consistently spent less than they earned and saved the rest. The year they both turned fifty-four, they sold their small business, and the money from the sale plus their savings has allowed them to serve in ministry without the need to receive a salary. Ask the Lord if He wants you to begin preparing yourself for the future to serve in a ministry as a part-time or full-time volunteer.

7. To open a business.

Another purpose for saving is to accumulate enough money to open and operate a business without going into debt. The amount of money will vary depending upon the requirements of each business.

As you can see, investing is about more than just making money. Just as purchasing an airplane ticket is not just for the enjoyment of flying but to get you to your desired destination, investments are vehicles to help you reach the real goals and dreams you have for your family. That's why having investments should never be an end within itself, but instead a means to the end. There may be more legitimate reasons to invest than what I have listed, but I have found that these seven are the most important to the people I have advised over the years.

SURE AND STEADY:
BASIC PRINCIPLES OF INVESTING

People who invest have the expectation of receiving income, growth in value, or a combination of the two. The purpose and intention of this book is not to recommend any specific investments. Obviously, being a professional investment adviser, my bias is toward financial securities like stocks, bonds, mutual funds, etc. However, because I don't know your individual situation, my objective is to draw your attention to the following scriptural frameworks for investing.

Be a steady plodder.

"Steady plodding brings prosperity; hasty speculation brings poverty" (Proverbs 21:5, TLB). The original Hebrew word for *steady plodding* pictures a person filling a large barrel one handful at a time. Little by little, the barrel is filled to overflowing. Examine various investments. Almost all of them are well suited for steady plodding. Your home mortgage is paid off after years of steady payments. A stock portfolio is built as it is added to each month, and a business can increase steadily in value through the years as its potential is developed.

Understand compound interest.

The amazingly wealthy Baron Rothschild was once asked if he had seen the Seven Wonders of the World. He is reported to have responded, "No, but I do know the advantages of the eighth wonder of the world—compound interest." Understanding how compounding works is very important. There are three variables in compounding: the amount you save, the interest rate you earn, and the length of time you save.

1. The Amount
    Your level of income and how much you spend for your living expenses and debt will always determine the amount you save. It is my hope that you will be able to increase the amount available for saving as you apply these biblical principles. Remember, high income does not equal wealth. Many famous athletes and entertainers who have made millions would agree with that. Dr. Will Norton modeled this principle. He served ten years as a missionary in Africa and earned only $250 a month. His salary supported his wife and their four young children. By growing much of their own food and spending wisely, they were able to purchase a house upon their return home to the Unied States with the money they saved.

2. Rate of Return
    The second factor is the rate of return you earn on an investment. The table on the next page shows how an investment of $1,000 a year grows at various interest rates.
    As you can see, the increase in the rate of interest has a remarkable impact on the amount accumulated. A 2 percent increase almost doubles the amount over forty years.

Saving and Investing

Interest	Year 5	Year 10	Year 20	Year 30	Year 40
6%	5,975	13,972	38,993	83,802	164,048
8%	6,336	15,645	49,423	122,346	279,781
10%	6,716	17,531	63,003	180,943	486,851
12%	7,115	19,655	80,699	270,293	859,142

Also, there is an investment law called the Rule of 72. Most people in the Black community have never heard of or been taught this simple rule. I'm always amazed that elementary, high school, and college curriculums teach us about calculus, geometry, and physics (stuff most of us will never use) and don't teach us about the Rule of 72. This rule is determined by taking seventy-two, then dividing it by the interest or rate of return, and the sum will equal the number of years to double your investment. For instance, if you earn 1 percent on your money, it will take seventy-two years for one dollar to become two dollars (seventy-two divided by 1 percent equals seventy-two years to double your investment). If you earned 10 percent on your money, it would take 7.2 years for one dollar to become two dollars (seventy-two divided by 10 percent equals 7.2 years to double your investment). On the next page, I have listed some other examples of the Rule of 72. However, as you look at what it will take to double your money, be careful not to make investments that are too risky in order to receive a high return. Usually the higher the rate, the higher the risk.

3. Time

The graph on page 176 may help you better visualize the benefits of starting now. If a person faithfully saves $2.74 each day—$1,000 per year—and earns 10 percent on the savings, at the end of forty years,

Rule 72

1%	=	72 years
4%	=	18 years
5%	=	14.4 years
6%	=	12 years
10%	=	7.2 years
12%	=	6 years
18%	=	4 years
24%	=	3 years

At a 12 percent return, $10,000.00 becomes:

$20,000.00	in	6 years
$40,000.00	in	2 years
$80,000.00	in	18 years
$160,000.00	in	24 years
$320,000.00	in	30 years
$640,000.00	in	36 years

the savings will grow to $486,000 and will be earning more than $4,000 each month in interest alone! However, if the person waits one year before starting, then saves for thirty-nine years, he will accumulate $45,260 less. Start saving today!

Avoid speculative investments.

"There is another serious problem I have seen everywhere—savings are put into risky investments that turn sour, and soon there is nothing left to pass on to one's son. The man who speculates is soon back to where he began—with nothing" (Ecclesiastes 5:13–15 TLB). Scripture warns of avoiding risky investments, yet each year thousands of people lose money in highly speculative and sometimes dishonest investments. How many times have you heard of people losing their life's savings on some get-rich-quick scheme? Sadly, it seems that many Christians are particularly vulnerable to such schemes because they trust others who appear to live by the same values as they do. We have known of investment scandals in churches, where "wolves in sheep's clothing fleeced the flock." Below are three characteristics that will help you identify a potentially risky investment:

1. You are offered an unusually high profit or interest rate that is "practically guaranteed."
2. The decision to invest must be made quickly. There will be no opportunity to investigate the investment or the promoter who is selling the investment. The promoter will often be doing you a "favor" by allowing you to invest.
3. Little will be said about the risks of losing money, and the investment will usually require no effort on your part. You may even be told that sometimes a portion of the profits will be "dedicated to the Lord's work."

Before participating in any investment, please be patient, and prayerfully do your homework.

The Early Bird Gets the Worm

Age	Individual A Contribution	Individual A Year-end Value	Individual B Contribution	Individual B Year-end Value
21	1,000	1,100	0	0
22	1,000	2,310	0	0
23	1,000	3,641	0	0
24	1,000	5,105	0	0
25	1,000	6,716	0	0
26	1,000	8,487	0	0
27	1,000	10,436	0	0
28	1,000	12,579	0	0
29	0	13,837	1,000	1,100
30	0	15,221	1,000	2,310
31	0	16,743	1,000	3,641
32	0	18,470	1,000	5,105
33	0	20,259	1,000	6,716
34	0	22,284	1,000	8,487
35	0	24,513	1,000	10,436
36	0	26,964	1,000	12,579
37	0	29,661	1,000	14,937
38	0	32,627	1,000	17,531
39	0	35,889	1,000	20,384
40	0	39,478	1,000	23,523
41	0	43,426	1,000	26,975
42	0	47,769	1,000	30,772
43	0	52,546	1,000	34,950
44	0	57,800	1,000	39,545
45	0	63,580	1,000	44,599
46	0	69,938	1,000	50,159
47	0	76,932	1,000	56,275
48	0	84,625	1,000	63,003
49	0	93,088	1,000	70,403
50	0	103,397	1,000	78,543
51	0	112,636	1,000	87,497
52	0	123,898	1,000	97,347
53	0	136,290	1,000	108,182
54	0	149,919	1,000	120,100
55	0	164,911	1,000	133,210
56	0	181,402	1,000	147,631
57	0	199,542	1,000	163,494
58	0	219,496	1,000	180,943
59	0	241,446	1,000	200,138
60	0	265,590	1,000	221,252
61	0	292,149	1,000	244,477
62	0	321,364	1,000	270,024
63	0	353,501	1,000	298,127
64	0	388,851	1,000	329,039
65	0	427,736	1,000	363,043
Total Investment	**$8,000**		**$37,000**	
Total Amount Accumulated	**$427,736**		**$363,043**	

Diversify.

"Divide your portion to seven, or even to eight, for you do not know what misfortune may occur on the earth" (Ecclesiastes 11:2). There is no guaranteed investment on this earth. Without proper diversification you can lose all of your money. I've known quite a few people who put all of their money into one stock because they were confident it was a "sure thing." My advice to people who want to do this has always been the same: "Don't do it." There are many horror stories I could share with you about people who lost all their money because they broke this simple principle.

Diversification can be compared to taking your bags to the car after grocery shopping. Let's say you have three different grocery bags and one of the bags contains eggs. If you drop the one with the eggs in it, then you've just destroyed all of your eggs. If you had put some of the eggs in the other two bags, you would still have some eggs that would be good. Hence, that's where we get the saying, "Don't put all your eggs in one basket." You never know what will happen to an investment either; all investments go through periods where they may drop, and therefore you need to diversify.

Count the cost.

With every investment there are costs—financial costs, time commitments, effort required, and sometimes even emotional stress. For example, the purchase of a rental house will require time and effort to lease and maintain. If the tenant is irresponsible, you may have to try to collect rent from someone who does not want to pay—talk about emotions! Before you decide on any investment, carefully consider all the costs.

Timing

"There is an appointed time for everything. And there is a time for every event under heaven" (Ecclesiastes 3:1). The right investment at the wrong time is the wrong investment. The decision to either purchase or sell an investment is best made prayerfully after seeking counsel.

Don't panic.

Sometimes you can have the appropriate investments and good advice but still experience a period of time where your investment produces a negative return. That doesn't necessarily mean that it is a bad investment. Sometimes you have to ride out negative cycles before things turn positive again. Cycles are a part of life; that's why you have to be properly diversified. The biggest enemies to building wealth through investments are greed and fear. Therefore, try not to be overly aggressive when your investments are doing well or panic when your investments go down.

INVESTMENTS TO CONSIDER

As I stated in a previous chapter, having a paycheck from a "good job" is not the best way to create wealth. You can't pass a "good job" down to the next generation. The key to creating wealth is spending less than you earn to create a surplus and then putting your money to work for you. Most of the wealthiest people in America produced their wealth by putting their money to work through securities (stocks, bonds, mutual funds), real estate, and business ownership. Since very few African-Americans are going to inherit millions of dollars, it behooves us to concentrate our efforts on these three areas. These are not the only areas one can invest in, but for this particular lesson, we'll limit our discussion to these three.

Please remember that no one investment is ideal for everyone. You should always invest your money based on your particular financial needs and risk tolerance.

1. Investing in securities

Stocks

A share of stock represents ownership in a company. A company issues stock to raise money for its business. Successful stock investors know that wealth comes from successful businesses and that the opportunity for personal wealth comes from owning part of these businesses.

Believe it or not, even though I am a veteran in the investment business, I didn't know what a stock was until I was a sophomore in college. When I was growing up, no one in my immediate family invested in stocks. Investing was just not a part of our dinner-table conversation. I knew about saving for emergencies, certificates of deposits, and passbook savings accounts, but blue-chip stocks and mutual funds were foreign concepts to me. The same was true for most of my friends and relatives. As a matter of fact, my ignorance about the stock market was pretty typical of most Black families I grew up around.

However, today times are different for me, my family, and African-Americans in general. A study done by Charles Schwab and Ariel Mutual Funds offers some encouraging news. More than half (57 percent) of African-Americans with household incomes of $50,000 or more (versus 81 percent of our White counterparts) have invested money in the stock market. That's good news, even though, as a culture overall, we still only invest 2 percent of our disposable income dollars in stocks.

I believe that in order for the African-American culture to move from a consumer-driven people to a producer-driven people, we need to consider the benefits that stock investing offers. As consumers, we've been making these companies rich for years. Now it's time for us to be on the other side of the table as investors instead of just being consumers.

The Dow Jones Industrial Average (DJIA) is by far the most popular indicator of general stock market direction; it is recognized and quoted worldwide. The DJIA represents the average stock price of thirty major blue-chip companies. Following is the list of companies on the index as of December 2000:

Alcoa Inc. (AA)	Eastman Kodak CO (EK)
American Express Co. (AXP)	Exxon Mobil Corp. (XOM)
AT & T Corp. (T)	General Electric Co. (GE)
Boeing Co. (BA)	General Motors Corp. (GM)
Caterpillar Inc. (CAT)	Home Depot Inc. (HD)
Citigroup Inc. (C)	Honeywell International Inc. (HON)
Coca-Cola Co. (KO)	Hewlett-Packard Co. (HEP)
Dupont Co. (DD)	IBM (IBM)

Intel Corp. (INTC)
International Paper Co. (IP)
J. P. Morgan & Co. (JPM)
Johnson & Johnson (JNJ)
McDonald's Corp. (MCD)
Merck & Co. (MRK)
Microsoft Corp. (MSFT)

Minnesota Mining
& Manufacturing (MMM)
Philip Morris Cos. (MO)
Proctor & Gamble Co. (PG)
SBC Communications Inc. (SBC)
United Technologies Corp. (UTX)
Wal-Mart Stores Inc. (WMT)
Walt Disney Co.

Think for a moment about a typical day in your life and how much you use some of these DJIA companies' products. Consider this example:

You wake up in the morning and brush your teeth with a toothpaste made by Procter & Gamble. Then you go to your kitchen and open a refrigerator made by General Electric, you make a call on your AT & T telephone, and then jump in your General Motors car, which has Goodyear tires on it. On the way to work, you gas up at Chevron or Exxon, and you stop by McDonald's for a quick breakfast. You finally get to work and turn on your IBM or Hewlett Packard computer, then hurry out of the office to go to the airport so you won't miss your flight to Disney. You stop by the drugstore to pick up Eastman Kodak film so you can take some pictures while you're out of town. When you finally get to the airport, you whip out your American Express card to pay for your flight. Then you get on an airplane made by Boeing. You have a headache from such a hectic day, so you take some medicine made by Merck or Johnson & Johnson.

OK, get the picture? All of the companies mentioned in this fictitious day are DJIA companies. Why not invest in them if you're going to be using their products? Remember, every time you spend money as a consumer on one of the products made by a DJIA company, you help their bottom line. Eventually, if a company continues to be profitable, it will ultimately reflect that profitability in a higher stock price.

Why invest in stocks? Historically, stocks are unmatched in their ability to grow and stay ahead of inflation over time. This makes them ideal investments for long-term goals, such as retirement and college education. Investors who have weathered stock-market fluctuations have earned returns far in excess of all other asset categories.

Bonds

Compared to stocks, bonds may not be glamorous or inspire banner headlines in your local newspaper. Still, bonds attract more investors than any other security. According to the Federal Reserve, in terms of dollar volume traded, the bond market is many times larger than the stock market.

What is a bond? A bond is a loan, or an IOU, in which the bond buyer lends money to the bond issuer. Because individual bonds offer a steady stream of interest income, they often are called fixed-income securities. Governments and corporations are the most common bond issuers.

Generally, bonds pay higher income than short-term instruments such as money-market funds, CDs, and savings accounts. For this reason, placing a portion of your savings into bonds is a popular strategy for investors who often use this income to help pay living expenses. Also, many investors lower their total income tax bill by placing a portion of their assets in municipal bonds. This provides them with income exempt from federal income taxes.

Mutual Funds

A mutual fund is a collection of stock, bond, or money market securities that is owned by many investors and managed by a professional investment company.

When you invest in a mutual fund, your dollars are pooled with other investors' dollars. The fund's management team uses that money to build and manage a portfolio of securities. Each fund has an investment objective or strategy that dictates, in general, what types of securities are bought for the fund's portfolio. Your investment buys shares of that portfolio at a share price that is updated daily.

When you invest in mutual funds, you can make money in one of three ways: 1) capital appreciation—the share price of your fund rises as the securities in its portfolio increase in market value; 2) capital gains—your fund sells securities for a profit, which your fund pays to you; or 3) dividend income—the securities in your fund's portfolio earn interest or pay you dividends.

The advantages of a mutual fund are: 1) *professional money management*—expert portfolio managers study the markets to make informed decisions on your behalf; 2) *diversification*—you are not dependent on one type of security or company in your portfolio; 3) *variety of investment choices*—you can choose a fund for whatever your objective is; 4) *low minimum investment*—many mutual funds minimums are as low as twenty-five dollars; and 5) *liquidity*—you can sell your shares at their current net asset value anytime, and the mutual fund companies are required to "buy back" your shares at your request.

2. *Investing in real estate*

Another popular way to invest is real estate. This can be done with residential real estate, commercial real estate, or raw land. There are always three main keys to successful real estate investing: location, location, location.

Food for thought: What Fortune 500 company is the largest single owner of real estate in the world? Believe it or not, it's McDonald's. Every McDonald's restaurant is sitting on prime real estate that the corporation owns. The corporation is not just in the fast-food business but also the real estate business.

Come to think of it, this whole planet is one big piece of real estate. From the time you get up until the time you go to sleep, you are walking, working, sitting, riding over, or lying down on somebody's real estate. Somebody is making money on virtually every house, store, office building, apartment complex, shopping center, or car wash that you see. Although real estate and land is plentiful, God is not making more of it. It's the only asset that cannot be reproduced. That's why real estate can be a valuable commodity.

Wars have been fought and lives have been lost over the control of land. You see, whoever owns the land has control over what happens in the community. That's why I believe that it is imperative that African-

American businesses, individuals, and especially churches own the land, buildings, and houses in our communities. Unfortunately, 60 to 90 percent of the property in the African-American community is owned by non-African-Americans.[3] Too many of us are tenants instead of landlords.

Owning land for African-Americans has always been a struggle. After slavery, President Abraham Lincoln and the Freedom Bureau, as compensation for 250 years of bondage, promised Africans forty acres of land, fifty dollars, and a mule. In 1866, President Andrew Johnson, who was Lincoln's vice president, along with the Southern states' encouragement, quickly canceled the congressional bill, and it has been somewhat of a real-estate nightmare for African-Americans ever since.

I vacation in Hilton Head, South Carolina, a lot. I love to go there and spend time with my family, eat good food, and play golf. A few years ago, someone gave me the history of Hilton Head, and it brought tears to my eyes. After slavery was over, Black people owned most of Hilton Head Island. Over the years, real-estate developers came in and converted the area into luxury estates and a vacation paradise. The property taxes that were levied against the African-Americans who lived there were so high and unfair that most of them were unable to pay them. The ones who could not pay were coerced into selling their property. African-Americans loved the area so much, they moved into smaller towns in the nearby area and were bused into Hilton Head to work on what are now called "Luxury Plantations."[4]

In most cases, African-Americans have a tough time trying to purchase homes for their families. Home ownership still is and has always been the hallmark of the "American Dream." It has been the single most important asset for accumulating wealth for most Americans. Families with modest to average amounts of wealth hold most of that wealth in their homes. According to authors Melvin Oliver and Thomas Shapiro in their book *Black Wealth, White Wealth*, 63 percent of all Black wealth and 43 percent of all White wealth is represented in home equity. The authors also noted that, in general, homes of similar design, size, and appearance cost more in White communities than in Black or integrated communities. Also, Whites tend to pay a premium to live in homogeneous neighborhoods, but their property appreciates at an enhanced rate. The authors deduced that the lower values of Black homes have adversely affected the ability of Blacks to utilize their residences as collateral for obtaining personal, business, or educational loans. Also, the valuing of neighborhoods based on race has contributed to the enormous wealth gaps between Black and White households. They estimate that decades of institutional biases in the residential areas have cost the current generation of African-Americans about $82 billion. Now that's a lot of money!—money that should have been circulating in our community but didn't because of racism.

Well, as you can see, this issue of land and real estate is important for Blacks and even more important for men and women of the kingdom. The largest investment and most serious financial decision most of us will ever make will probably involve real estate.

I'll leave you with this example of why acquiring land is more of a kingdom cause than a financial issue. My good friend Dr. Tony Evans is pastor of Oak Cliff Bible Fellowship in Dallas. Over the past twenty years, he has gradually acquired more than one hundred acres of land that surround the church's property. While visiting with him one day, I asked him what his plans were for some of the newly acquired property. He told me that there are three reasons his church has aggressively acquired the property around them: 1) for ministry; 2) for investment; and 3) control. He said, "Lee, as long as we own this property, it will be used for the kingdom purposes today and for generations to come." Now that's what kingdom investing is all about. That's also the beauty of real estate.

3. Investing in your own business

One of the best ways to become wealthy is to invest in a business that you own. As I stated earlier, for every one thousand members of the African-American culture there are nine businesses, while in the larger White community there are sixty-four businesses per one thousand.[5]

We first need more people in our culture to step out in faith and become entrepreneurs. Statistics say that 38 percent of the people that are wealthy got that way through owning their own business.[6]

Entrepreneurship allows you the opportunity to pass greater wealth to your children. It also allows your children the opportunity to learn the business and eventually own it.

The biggest challenge for those that own their own business is what to do with profits. The most common mistake I see among African-American business owners is that they rob themselves of the necessary capital their businesses need by buying expensive personal items.

Now, don't get me wrong. I am a business owner, too, and I believe in rewarding myself. Most entrepreneurs work longer and harder now than they did while working for someone else. The problem is this: If you don't significantly invest in your business but instead buy your "much-deserved" BMW or Mercedes, you could actually be hurting your business. That money you spent trying to impress people and show them how "successful" you are could have been capital to take your business to the next level. I am not saying you should take an oath of poverty, but balance and moderation are essential.

Remember this: *If you feed your business what it needs now, it will feed you what you need later.*

GAMBLING AND LOTTERIES

Lotteries and gambling of all types are sweeping our country. Three hundred billion dollars a year is spent on gambling. Whether it is playing cards in a friend's home, visiting a casino, or buying a lottery ticket at the corner market, gambling touches all of us at some point. Some people believe the only way to get rich is to win the lottery. I have heard people say, "That's my only hope out of this mess." That is why most lottery outlets are located among the disfranchised. The lottery is aimed at the poor and financed by the poor. When I stop at convenience stores in these areas in Atlanta, the lines to buy lottery tickets are always very long. I've had many people tell me they can't save money, but they spend $50 a month on lottery tickets. Over a period of twenty years, that would be a loss of $12,000, and, believe me, that money will be lost. You have a better chance of striking oil in your backyard or being hit by lightning —twice—than you do of winning the lottery.

But if that same $12,000 was invested at 20 percent interest over those twenty years, this person would have $34,365. I think the wisdom of investing instead of playing the lottery speaks for itself.

To make sure people play the lottery, the promoters parade some winner in front of the television holding a huge check for four or five million. You don't have to be poor to start salivating when lottery officials tell you the next winner could be you. Consider this: When a poor person plays the lottery, every dollar he gives to the lottery is a dollar less for food on his table, rent money, heat in the winter, and clothes for the kids. Every time he gives a dollar to the lottery, that's one dollar less he has to get out of the situation his family is in. If you're playing the lottery and you are not poor, you are helping support and feed a system that is ripping off poor people. As long as able-bodied people are looking to the government for their livelihoods, our communities will be handicapped.

As far as Christians are concerned, a recent study discovered that people spend fifteen times more money on gambling than they donate to churches! The average church member gives $20 a year to foreign missions while the average person gambles at least $1,174 annually. Hundreds of thousands are compulsive gamblers who regularly lose their family's income. The stories are heartbreaking. One who participates in gambling or lotteries usually does so in an attempt to get rich quick. This is a violation of Scripture. "He who makes haste to be rich will not go unpunished" (Proverbs 28:20). "A man with an evil eye hastens after wealth and does not know that want will come upon him" (Proverbs 28:22).

So what is the bottom line? Not all gambling, or risk-taking, is wrong. Going to an amusement park and paying a dollar to try to win a teddy bear is not wrong. But any form of gambling that violates biblical principles is certainly a bad bet!

THE ONE GUARANTEED INVESTMENT

I was nineteen years old when I attended a meeting for my college football team. I was very impressed with the speaker. He spoke about how we could be better athletes and students. After the meeting, this speaker, a former pro football player, spoke about his relationship with Christ. His background was very similar to mine. At that time I was a popular star athlete, good student, and most of my peers admired me. I had everything I thought would give me happiness and a sense of accomplishment, but I had neither. Something was missing in my life. I was surprised to hear this successful businessman and former athlete speak openly of his faith in God. I grew up going to church regularly but missed hearing about a personal relationship with Jesus Christ. A friend described how I could enter into this relationship with the Lord. He taught me five biblical truths that I had never before understood.

1. God loves you and wants you to know Him and experience a meaningful life.

God desires an intimate relationship with each of us. My friend directed my attention to two passages: "For God so loved the world, that He gave His only begotten Son, that whoever believes in Him shall not perish, but have eternal life" (John 3:16). "I [Jesus] came that they may have life, and may have it abundantly" (John 10:10).

I have two sons, Martin and Ryan. Although I love other people, I do not love others enough to give either of my sons to die for them. But that is how much God the Father loves you. He gave His only Son, Jesus Christ, to die for you.

2. Unfortunately, we are separated from God.

My friend asked if I had ever sinned, ever done anything that would disqualify me from being perfect. "Many times," I admitted. He explained that every person has sinned, and sin separates us from God. "For all have sinned and fall short of the glory of God" (Romans 3:23). "Your sins have cut you off from God" (Isaiah 59:2 TLB).

A gap separates people from God. Individuals try without success to bridge this gap through their own efforts, such as philosophy, religion, or living a good, moral life.

3. God's only provision to bridge this gap is Jesus Christ.

Jesus Christ died on the cross to pay the penalty for our sin and bridge the gap from people to God. Jesus said, "I am the way, and the truth, and the life; no one comes to the Father, but through Me" (John 14:6). "But God demonstrates His own love toward us, in that while we were yet sinners, Christ died for us" (Romans 5:8).

4. This relationship is a gift from God.

My friend explained that by an act of faith, I could receive the free gift of a relationship with God. "For by grace you have been saved through faith; and that not of yourselves, it is the gift of God; not as a result of works, so that no one may boast" (Ephesians 2:8–9).

5. We must each receive Jesus Christ individually.

I had only to repent of my sins and ask Jesus Christ to come into my life as Savior and Lord. And I did it. As my friends will tell you, I am a very practical person. If something does not work, I stop doing it quickly. I can tell you from over twenty years' experience that a relationship with the living God is available to you through Jesus Christ. Nothing I know of compares with knowing Christ personally. If you desire to know the Lord and are not certain whether you have this relationship, I encourage you to receive Christ right now. Pray a prayer similar to this one: "Father God, I need You. I invite Jesus to come into my life as my Savior and Lord and make me the person You want me to be. Thank You for forgiving my sins and giving me the gift of eternal life. Amen." You might apply each of the principles to become a faithful steward, but without a relationship with Christ, our efforts will be worth nothing. If you ask Christ into your life, please tell someone you know who can assist you in your spiritual growth.

Chapter Nine

—ⱷ ⱷ—

DIVIDENDS
OF HONESTY
AND INTEGRITY

$\mathcal{O}$ne day, a pastor of a church decided to go shopping on his day off. After choosing what he wanted in his favorite store, he approached the counter to pay for his merchandise. He gave the cash register attendant a couple of hundred-dollar bills, and she gave him back some change.

When the pastor got to his car, he noticed that the cash register attendant had given him too much change. According to his calculations, she overpaid him by ten dollars. The pastor agonized over what he should do next. *Should I return the money, or should I keep the money?* he asked himself. After a while he began to rationalize why he should keep the money. He thought, *Surely, a big department store like this won't miss ten dollars. They don't need the money like I do.* Finally, the pastor decided to return the money to the store.

When he approached the lady at the cash register, he said, "Excuse me, but you made a mistake when you gave me my change back. You overpaid me by ten dollars." The lady at the cash register told him,

"Sir, I did not make a mistake. You see, I was at your church last Sunday when you preached a message on honesty and integrity—I just wanted to see whether or not you practiced what you preached."

All of us have to make daily decisions about whether or not to handle money honestly. Do you tell the cashier at the grocery store when you receive too much change? Have you ever tried to sell something and been tempted not to tell the whole truth because you might have lost the sale? Have you lied on your income tax returns?

HONESTY IN SOCIETY

I truly believe that what we do with our money says more about our character than anything else. I've met people that I have liked and respected until I started to do business with them. That's when I saw their true character. Money always brings out the real us.

Many people ask me, "Lee, do you have to be honest and have integrity to be wealthy?" I usually respond by saying, "No, you can become wealthy without being a person of honesty and integrity, but you can't stay wealthy that way." I've seen many in the investment profession lie and cheat their way to the top, only to lose their big houses and cars after their fraudulent acts were found out. Moral decisions, whether good or bad, always have economic consequences.

These decisions are made more difficult because we live in what has been called the "Age of the Rip-off." It is a time when employee theft is approaching $1 billion a week! It is a time when almost everyone around us seems to be acting dishonestly.

People make up their own standards of honesty that change depending upon their circumstances. Judges 17:6 says, "Every man did what was right in his own eyes." Some of us who are African-Americans find it easy to justify cheating on taxes and buying stolen goods because we feel that the system hasn't treated us fairly and never will. When some of us get the opportunity to get over on Mr. Charlie, we do it with no regret.

Jerome Smith is twenty-four years old and serving time in prison for robbery. He explains, "I just lost hope. I had been fired and had become very angry. The only way I figured I could get ahead was by steal-ing and selling stolen goods. When I got caught, I lost my freedom and my future." People don't realize how much dishonesty can hurt them financially. It will be so much harder for Jerome to get a good job with a prison record.

Dishonesty also harms the entire community, because part of a store's price markup is to cover the cost of shoplifting and employee theft. That's why prices are higher in lower-income areas than higher-income areas. The people who can least afford to pay the higher prices have to because of the theft that goes on in these areas.

HONESTY IN SCRIPTURE

God demands absolute honesty. Proverbs 20:23 reads, "The Lord loathes all cheating and dishonesty" (TLB). And Proverbs 12:22 states, "Lying lips are an abomination to the Lord." And from Proverbs 6:16–17 we read, "The Lord hates . . . a lying tongue." Study the comparison on the next page between what the Scriptures teach and what our so-ciety practices concerning honesty.

The God of truth

Truthfulness is one of God's unchangeable characteristics. He is repeatedly identified as the God of truth. "I am . . . the truth" (John 14:6). Moreover, the Lord commands us to reflect His honest and holy char-acter: "Be holy yourselves also in all your behavior; because it is written, 'You shall be holy, for I am holy'" (1 Peter 1:15–16).

In contrast to God's nature, Jesus describes the devil's character: "He [the devil] was a murderer from the beginning, and does not stand in the truth because there is no truth in him. Whenever he speaks a lie, he speaks from his own nature, for he is a liar and the father of lies" (John 8:44)

The Lord wants us to become conformed to His honest character rather than to the dishonest nature of the devil.

Honesty & Integrity

Issue	Scripture	Society
Standard of honesty:	Absolute	Relative
God's concern about honesty:	He demands honesty	There is no God
The decision to be honest or dishonest is based upon:	Faith in the invisible living God	Only what I can see
Question usually asked deciding whether to be honest:	Will it please God?	Will I get away with it?

Absolute honesty

God has imposed the standard of absolute honesty for Christians for the following reasons:

1. We Cannot Practice Dishonesty and Love God.

Two of the Ten Commandments address honesty. "You shall not steal. You shall not bear false witness against your neighbor" (Exodus 20:15–16). And Jesus told us, "If you love Me, you will keep My commandments" (John 14:15). According to Scripture, we cannot practice dishonesty and still love God. A dishonest person acts as if God does not even exist! When we act dishonestly, we believe that God is not able to provide what we need, even though He has promised to do so (Matthew 6:33). So we decide to take things into our own hands and do it our own dishonest way.

A dishonest person is also acting as if God is incapable of discovering our dishonesty and is powerless to discipline us. If we really believe God will discipline us, then we will not consider acting dishonestly.

Honest behavior is an issue of faith. An honest decision may look foolish in light of what we can see. But the godly person knows Jesus Christ is alive. Every honest decision strengthens our faith in God and helps us grow into a closer relationship with Christ. However, if we choose to be dishonest, we really are denying our Lord. It is impossible to love God with all our hearts, souls, and minds if at the same time we are dishonest and act as if He does not exist. Scripture declares that the dishonest hate God. "He who walks in his uprightness fears the Lord, but he who is crooked in his ways despises Him" (Proverbs 14:2).

Early in my investment career, I worked with a large investment firm that grossly overpaid me on some commissions I had earned. When I called the payroll department to tell them about their mistake, the person in payroll told me they never would have discovered their error if I hadn't said anything about it. At first I felt stupid for being honest with them, especially knowing I could have gotten away with having an extra two thousand dollars. But I knew I did the right thing by telling the truth. Furthermore, I believed God was capable of allowing me to earn two thousand dollars the right way. Not long after I made the decision to report the two thousand dollars, I had a record month! Maybe that was a test for me. What about you? Did you pass your latest honesty test?

2. We Cannot Practice Dishonesty and Love Our Neighbor.

The Lord demands absolute honesty because dishonest behavior also violates the second commandment: "Thou shalt love thy neighbor as thyself" (Mark 12:31 KJV). Romans 13:9–10 reads, "If you love your neighbor as much as you love yourself you will not want to harm or cheat him, or kill him or steal from him. . . . Love does no wrong to anyone" (TLB).

When we act dishonestly, we are stealing from another person. We may deceive ourselves into thinking it is a business, the government, or an insurance company that is suffering loss, but really it is the business owners, fellow taxpayers, or the policyholders from whom we are stealing. It is just as if we took the money from their wallets. Dishonesty always injures people. The victim is always a person.

3. Honesty Creates Credibility for Evangelism.

Our Lord demands absolute honesty in handling money to enable us to demonstrate the reality of Jesus Christ to those who do not yet know Him.

I will never forget the time I shared my faith with a co-worker. He angrily responded, "Well, I know a man who always goes to church and talks a lot about Jesus. But you have to watch out for him at work. He's so dishonest that he'd cheat his own grandmother. If that's what it means to be a Christian, I don't want any part of it!" Our actions speak louder than our words. "Prove yourselves to be blameless and inno-cent, children of God above reproach in the midst of a crooked and per-verse generation, among whom you appear as lights in the world" (Philippians 2:15).

We can influence people for Jesus Christ by handling our money honestly. My friend Howard Dayton, in his book *Your Money Counts*, tells the story of his friend Robert who had been trying to sell an old car for months. Finally, an interested buyer decided to purchase the car. However, at the last moment he said, "I'll buy this car, but only on one condition: that you don't report this sale so I won't have to pay state sales tax." Although he was tempted, Robert responded, "I'm sorry, but I can't do that because Jesus Christ is my Lord." Robert later said, "You should have seen that man's reaction. He almost went into shock! Then an interesting thing happened. His attitude completely changed. Not only did he purchase the car, but he eagerly joined my wife and me around our dinner table. Rarely have I seen anyone as open to the truth about knowing Jesus Christ in a personal way." Because Robert had acted honestly even though it was going to cost him money, he had demon-strated to this person the reality of a personal faith in Jesus Christ.

4. Honesty Confirms God's Direction.

Proverbs 4:24–26 reads, "Put away from you a deceitful mouth and put devious lips far from you. Let your eyes look directly ahead and let your gaze be fixed straight in front of you. Watch the path of your feet and all your ways will be established."

What a tremendous principle. As you are absolutely honest, "all your ways will be established." Choosing to walk the narrow path of honesty eliminates the many possible avenues of dishonesty. Decision-making becomes simpler because the honest path is a clear path.

"If only I had understood that truth," one of my good friends named Raymond wept. "But Maria and I wanted that house so much. It was our dream home. However, our existing debts were so large that we couldn't qualify for the mortgage. The only way for us to buy the house was to hide some of our debts from the bank. It was the worst decision of my life. Almost immediately we were unable to meet the house payment and pay our other debts, too. The pressure built and was almost more than Maria could stand. Our dream house ended up causing a family nightmare. I not only lost the home, but I nearly lost my wife."

Had Raymond and Maria been honest, the bank would not have approved the loan. They would not have been able to purchase that particular home. Had they prayed and waited, perhaps the Lord would have brought something more affordable to their attention. This would have saved them from the stress that almost ended their marriage. Honesty helps confirm God's direction.

5. Even the Smallest Act of Dishonesty Is Harmful.

God requires us to be absolutely honest, because even the smallest act of dishonesty is sin. And even the smallest sin interrupts our fellowship with the Lord. The smallest "white lie" will harden our hearts, making our conscience increasingly insensitive to sin. This single cancer cell of small dishonesty multiplies and spreads to greater dishonesty. "Whoever is dishonest with very little will also be dishonest with much" (Luke 16:10 NIV).

One of my cousins got a job as a car salesman at a dealership. Because of his background, it was a miracle that he was able to get the job. Although he was a great salesman, he had been in and out of jail for minor infractions, but we believed he had finally learned his lesson. We encouraged him to be a good employee, because that job could lead to greater opportunities. In the first few months, he was awarded the honor of salesman of the month. He was finally making the kind of money of which he had dreamed. Then he called me one day and informed me that he had been fired because, he said, "A customer came in and purchased a car from me for twenty-five hundred dollars cash. When I wrote up the paperwork, I did it for twenty-four hundred dollars instead of twenty-five hundred dollars. I pocketed the other one hundred dollars for myself." I couldn't believe my cousin lost his job over one hundred dollars. I told him, "Man, if you needed a hundred bucks, I could have given it to you!" A hundred-dollar mistake cost him his job and a bright future.

An event in Abraham's life has challenged me to be honest in small matters. In Genesis 14 the king of Sodom offered Abraham all the goods Abraham recovered when he returned from successfully rescuing the people of Sodom. But Abraham responded to the king, "I have sworn to the Lord God Most High, possessor of heaven and earth, that I will not take a thread or a sandal thong or anything that is yours" (Genesis 14:22–23).

Just as Abraham was unwilling to take so much as a thread or a sandal thong, I challenge you to make a similar commitment in this area of honesty. Commit not to steal a stamp or a meal or a paper clip or a long-distance telephone call or a penny from your employer or anyone else. The people of God must be honest in even the smallest matters.

How to be honest

The character of our human nature is to act dishonestly. "Out of men's hearts, come evil thoughts . . . theft . . . deceit" (Mark 7:21–22 NIV). The desire of the Spirit is for us to be absolutely honest. I can't overemphasize that the absolutely honest life is supernatural. We must submit ourselves entirely to Jesus Christ as Lord and allow Him to live His life through us. There is no other way. Here are four things that can help:

1. Obey the Golden Rule.

"Do not merely look out for your own personal interests, but also for the interests of others" (Philippians 2:4). This verse is better translated, "look intently after the interests of others." The Lord confronted

196

me through this passage and pointed out my self-centeredness and lack of concern for others my first year in the investment business.

I got a call from this man who wanted to invest a very large sum of money with me. The problem was that he wanted to put all of the money in a complicated strategy called options. With this particular strategy, the investor can make a killing—or lose all of his money. It's a very risky strategy, but the commissions are great. I accepted the account knowing that I didn't feel comfortable with this style of investing, and knowing that this was not my area of expertise. I filled out the paperwork, and we were set to start the transactions the next day. The client knew nothing about my lack of expertise in this area. I did not tell him, because I needed the money.

After some serious inner struggles that night, I called the client before the stock market opened and told him the truth. I recommended that he use a more experienced adviser for this type of strategy. Practicing the Golden Rule cost me some serious commissions that day, but my reward was a clear conscience before God and other people. I slept very well the next night.

2. Fear the Lord.

When I talk of a "healthy fear" of the Lord, I do not mean that God is a big bully just waiting for the opportunity to punish us. He is rather a loving Father who, out of love, disciplines His children for their own good. "He disciplines us for our good, so that we may share His holiness" (Hebrews 12:10).

One of the ways God motivates us to honest living is this "healthy fear." Proverbs 16:6 reads, "By the fear of the Lord one keeps away from evil." Let me illustrate an embarrassing story of how the fear of the Lord helped me act honestly. My freshman year on the University of Tennessee football team was exciting. When we traveled, we always stayed in five-star hotels. On my very first trip with the team we stayed at a hotel that had some very nice glasses in the room. Most of the guys were stealing the glasses and the towels too. You know what they say— you can take the person out of the ghetto, but . . . Anyway, while I was packing to go back home after the game I slipped one of the hotel's drinking glasses into my suitcase and begin to zip up my bag. Suddenly I felt the fear of the Lord. I got that glass out of that suitcase so fast!

3. Don't Expect God's Blessings on Stolen Property.

I believe our heavenly Father will not allow us to keep anything we have acquired dishonestly. Proverbs 13:11 reads, "Wealth obtained by fraud dwindles." A friend told me that she had purchased a television and a stereo that she knew were hot (stolen items). She went on to say it was simply miraculous how quickly they broke and became worthless! Think about this for a moment: If you are a parent and one of your children shoplifts an item, do you allow the child to keep it? Of course not. You will return it because the child's character would be destroyed if he kept stolen property. Not only would you insist upon its return, but you would also want the child to experience enough pain so he wouldn't do it again. For instance, you might have the child confess the theft to the store manager. When our heavenly Father lovingly disciplines us, it is usually done in such a way that we will not forget. This can be painful or embarrassing.

4. Stay Away from Dishonest People.

Scripture teaches that we are deeply influenced by those around us, either for good or evil. Paul wrote, "Do not be deceived: Bad company corrupts good morals" (1 Corinthians 15:33). Solomon was even stronger: "He who is a partner with a thief hates his own life" (Proverbs 29:24).

Obviously, we cannot isolate ourselves from every dishonest person. In fact, we are to be salt and light in the world. We should, however, be very cautious when choosing our close friends.

It is much easier to be absolutely honest if you are surrounded by others who are also committed to being honest. If I see a person who is dishonest in his dealings with the government or in a small matter, I know this person will be dishonest in greater matters and probably in his dealings with me.

Dealing with dishonesty

Unfortunately, from time to time we will act dishonestly, but once we recognize that we have, we need to do the following:

1. We Must Restore Our Fellowship with God.

Anytime we sin, we break our fellowship with our Lord. This needs to be restored. First John 1:9 tells us how: "If we confess our sins, He is faithful and righteous to forgive us our sins and to cleanse us from all unrighteousness." We must agree with God that our dishonesty was sin and then thankfully accept God's gracious forgiveness so we can again enjoy His fellowship.

2. We Must Restore Our Fellowship with the Harmed Person.

After our fellowship with Christ has been restored, we need to confess our dishonesty to the person we offended. "Confess your sins to one another" (James 5:16). Confession helps break the habit of dishonesty.

Violating this principle may cause a person's lack of financial prosperity. "He who conceals his transgressions will not prosper, but he who confesses and forsakes them will find compassion" (Proverbs 28:13).

3. We Must Return Any Dishonestly Acquired Property.

If we have acquired anything dishonestly, we must return it to its rightful owner. "Then it shall be, when he sins and becomes guilty that he shall restore what he took by robbery . . . or anything about which he swore falsely; he shall make restitution for it in full, and add to it one-fifth more. He shall give it to the one to whom it belongs" (Leviticus 6:4–5).

Restitution is a tangible expression of repentance and an effort to correct a wrong. Zaccheus is a good example. He promised Jesus, "If I have defrauded anyone of anything, I will give back four times as much" (Luke 19:8). If it's not possible for restitution to be made, then the property should be given to the Lord. Numbers 5:8 teaches, "But if the man has no relative to whom restitution may be made for the wrong, the restitution which is made for the wrong must go to the Lord for the priest."

CHEAPENED INTEGRITY: BRIBES

A bribe is defined as anything given to a person to influence him to do something illegal or wrong. All too often we hear of someone in business or politics who is arrested for bribery. The taking of bribes is clearly prohibited in Scripture: "You shall not take a bribe, for a bribe blinds the clear-sighted and subverts the cause of the just" (Exodus 23:8). Bribes are often disguised as a "gift." Evaluate any such offer to confirm that it is not in reality a bribe.

HONESTY IN LEADERSHIP

All of us will serve in positions of leadership, either in work, at church, or as a parent. The Lord is especially concerned with the honesty of leaders.

Influence of leaders

Leaders influence those who follow them. The pastor of a church began wearing a particular style of suit. Within six months, most of the men at the church were wearing the same style suit. He suddenly changed to a different style, and six months later, most of the men were wearing the new style, too.

In a similar way, a dishonest leader produces dishonest followers. "If a ruler pays attention to falsehood, all his ministers become wicked" (Proverbs 29:12).

Selection of leaders

Dishonesty should disqualify a person from leadership. Listen to the counsel of Jethro, Moses' father-in-law: "You shall select out of all the people able men who fear God, men of truth, those who hate dishonest gain; and you shall place these . . . as leaders of thousands, of hundreds, of fifties and of tens" (Exodus 18:21).

Two of the four criteria for leadership selection that Jethro gave

Moses dealt with honesty: "men of truth" and "those who hate dishonest gain." I believe the Lord wants us to continue to select leaders on the basis of these same character qualities. This is especially true for those who serve in spiritual leadership in the church. This is the big question for you to answer: Am I going to be committed to living an absolutely honest life that will please God and influence others? You will be tempted often to compromise. It will require courage. If you want to make this commitment, there is no better time to start than right now.

Blessings and curses

Listed below are some of the blessings the Lord has promised for the honest and some of the curses reserved for the dishonest. Read these slowly and prayerfully, asking God to use His Word to motivate you to a life of honesty.

Blessings Promised for the Honest
Intimacy with the Lord. "For the crooked man is an abomination to the Lord; but He is intimate with the upright" (Proverbs 3:32).
A blessed family. "A righteous man who walks in his integrity—how blessed are his sons after him" (Proverbs 20:7).
Long life. "Truthful lips will be established forever, but a lying tongue is only for a moment." (Proverbs 12:19).
Prosperity. "Much wealth is in the house of the righteous, but trouble is in the income of the wicked" (Proverbs 15:6).

Curses Reserved for the Dishonest
Alienation from God. "For the crooked man is an abomination to the Lord" (Proverbs 3:32).
Family problems. "He who profits illicitly troubles his own house" (Proverbs 15:27).
Death. "The getting of treasures by a lying tongue is a fleeting vapor, the pursuit of death" (Proverbs 21:6).
Poverty. "Wealth obtained by fraud dwindles" (Proverbs 13:11).

Chapter Ten

INVESTING IN YOUR FAMILY

The greatest Father's Day gift I have ever received came from my older son, Martin. I was driving him home from baseball practice the day before Father's Day, and I asked him what he wanted to be when he grew up. He thought for a few moments; then he said, "Dad . . . I want to be just like you." Needless to say, my heart just melted. I wanted him to be specific, so I asked, "Why do you want to be like me?" His answer not only surprised me, but it showed me what's really important to children. I thought he was going to say he wanted to be like me because I played college and pro football, and he wanted to do that, too. Or that he wanted to be like me because I had a good business career and wore a suit and tie to work every day. Or that I served in the church and traveled throughout the country speaking to thousands of people. But he didn't say any of those things. He just looked at me and said, "I want to be like you because you're a good dad. You spend time with me and I'm going to do the same thing with my son."

By this time tears had welled up in my eyes because I was so touched by what my son told me. What's interesting is that he didn't say I was a good dad because I bought him toys or because of any material comforts I have provided for him. He said it was because I spent time with him, and what he saw in me he was going to emulate with his son one day.

This is not to say that I have been a perfect dad, because I haven't. I have three children and a wonderful wife, and I have made my mistakes. However, whenever I've blown it, I have never been too proud to humble myself and ask for their forgiveness. One thing I have always realized is that family is very, very important. I won't allow business, golf, or even church activities to cause me to neglect my family.

No matter how much you love God, a healthy family life doesn't just happen. It is the result of deliberate intention, determination, and choices. The Lord wants those of us who are parents and grandparents to leave a godly legacy to our offspring that becomes multigenerational. We must realize that what we do with our time, our treasures (money), and our talents today will directly influence the multigenerational cycle of family traits, beliefs, and actions—for good or for bad.

THE MULTIGENERATIONAL GOD

It is remarkable to read through Scripture and note how consistently God takes a multigenerational approach. From the judgment on Cain and his descendants, to the promise to Noah and all successive generations, to the covenant with Abraham and his seed, to the genealogies recorded in the Gospels, God is always looking forward with a view to your descendants. Throughout Scripture, the promises of God are consistently spoken of in terms of a generational blessing on your children and your children's children.

In the book of Hebrews, Esau was condemned as a godless person who "sold his own birthright for a single meal" (Hebrews 12:16). What was so "godless" about it all was that Esau lived only for the pressing needs of the moment, without concern for the blessings that would be transmitted to his descendants for dozens of generations. His failure was impatience and shortsightedness. In a similar way, the African-American culture has become shortsighted by mortgaging our future to have what we want right now.

According to a recent Black investor survey by Ariel Mutual Funds and Charles Schwab & Company, affluent African-Americans spend more money on car payments than they invest in their children's education. Unfortunately, this ego-driven, conspicuous consumption is occurring at our children's expense, and it is unbiblical. The Bible says parents ought to store up wealth for their children. That means a portion of what you accumulate belongs to your children, not to you.

Remember, God is the God of Abraham, Isaac, and Jacob. When God looks at you, He sees in you three generations. Therefore, what you do with your money should have generational repercussions. But most of us don't think that way. What's keeping many Black families poor is single-generation consumption. We are spending all that we have and are leaving basically nothing for the next generation to manage and continue to build. Our children and grandchildren are starting from scratch, unlike other cultures that pass wealth down from generation to generation. African-Americans are at least a generation behind when it comes to inheriting wealth. Less than 1 percent of Black baby boomers' wealth comes from inheritance, compared to 10 percent of their White counterparts, according to a Cornell University study. And future prospects look slim: 94 percent of Black couples age thirty-five to fifty-four don't expect to get an inheritance, compared with 70 percent of Whites. Blacks over the age of fifty-five—the group likely to hand down assets—have about one-fourth the wealth of their White counterparts.

On the other hand, as many Christians begin to see things from God's perspective, we will start to think eternally and to act multi-generationally. We will start to invest our time, effort, and money in such a way that it will be a blessing to our children, even to the fourth generation and beyond. As a general rule, whatever God builds endures at least three generations. And as a rule, it takes at least three generations for a major character trait to be implanted, or replaced, in a family.[1] As African-Americans, we need to start replacing consumption with savings, and selfishness with heritage.

I want to challenge you to look beyond the immediate to consider how you can help set in motion a tradition that will establish a legacy of financial faithfulness in your family or with those you love. If you are not married or have no children, you may have an opportunity to influence nephews or nieces. If you are a grandparent, you have the privilege of touching the second generation by helping to train your grandchildren.

CONTROVERSY, CIRCUMSTANCES, AND THE BLACK FAMILY

One of the most publicly maligned institutions in America has been the Black family. Leaders ranging from politicians and educators to clergy and Black activists have bemoaned the absence of Black men from the family, the hardships endured by Black mothers, the economic woes of Black families, and the breakdown of the extended family in the African-American community.[2]

While there are many solid, happy African-American families, there is no avoiding the cold facts. Over the last few decades, there has been a continued erosion of traditional family ties and strength. In 1959, 2 percent of Black children were raised in households where the mother never married.[3] Today, government statistics indicate that roughly two out of every three Black children (66 percent) born this year will be born to a mother who is not married. Of the eight million Black families in this country, less than half (46 percent) are married.

While the good news is that the dissolution of Black families seems to have plateaued over the last several years, the bad news is that a majority of Black children under the age of eighteen are living with a single parent. In 93 percent of those situations, that parent is the mother—who in most cases receives no child support payments from her former husband (or boyfriend), and a large proportion of whom struggle to make ends meet financially. Slightly more than one out of every four Black families lives in poverty—more than double the proportion among Caucasian families.[4]

Clearly, being Black in America is not easy. We must remeber that we are only five generations removed from slavery. According to Bishop

T. D. Jakes, in his terrific book *The Great Investment: Faith, Family, and Finances,* he states that one of the most damaging aspects of slavery was not the beatings—though they were horrendous. It was not the murders, as reprehensible as they were. The greatest atrocity, the one that had the strongest repercussions, was the loss of the family unit. Just a century ago, African-American families did not exist, and loyalty to a woman or child was disallowed. Jakes goes on to say, "Our men were rewarded for making babies they weren't allowed to keep. Our children were crops to be sold at the auctions, and our wives were whoever would bear the greatest harvest." Regardless of how so many millions of African-American people arrived in their difficult family circumstances, the inescapable fact is that somehow we have managed to get through the hardships and make the most out of our situations. We are a strong people. One of the foundations of that strength and resiliency is our faith in God. We have truly come this far by faith. We know that God is still interested in the family, and He wants our home to succeed.

THE MARRIED COUPLE

God first instituted marriage when he created Adam and Eve. The first family unit consisted of the husband, the wife, and their offspring (Genesis 2:19–24; 4:1–2). Therefore, marriage has always been important to God as well as to the African-American people. It represents one of the most sacred bonds two people can make. A few generations ago, a couple couldn't even date seriously unless they had their wedding plans in place. Living together, eloping, and getting married without the sanction of family was never looked upon favorably in African-American culture. Today, most Black folks still expect their children to become family the old-fashioned way—standing up before family and loved ones in a house of worship or other spiritual environment—before they get pregnant. Even during slavery, marriage was a highly valued institution. While slave marriages were not legally recognized, they were acknowledged by fellow slaves and frequently sanctioned by slave owners. The slaves even created their own legitimate rituals like "jumping the broom."

Today, economics play a key role in marital satisfaction of Black couples. The saying that "there can't be any romance without finance" is definitely true. According to minister and family counselor Clarence Walker, the more satisfied wives are with their economic situation, the more satisfied they are with their marriage. The more contented Black husbands are with job rewards, the more likely they are to maintain their marriage. In the African-American culture, the revival of marriage may be the best anti-poverty strategy around. In a two-parent family, the probability that the family will be poor in any given year is 5 percent; for a single mother, the probability goes up to 50 percent.[5] That means that a Black single parent is ten times more likely to be poor than a Black married couple. The obvious reason for this is that married households can send more than one person into the labor force, but studies have shown that married couples also fare much better than single-headed households, even when only one partner works.

Also, the married couple seems to be the rule among White families and the exception among Blacks. Nearly 83 percent of White families are built around married couples, compared with 46 percent of Black families.[6] Most economists and demographers believe this is one of the reasons that such a wide wealth gap exists between Blacks and Whites.

But just because marriages may be the most "economically successful" family type doesn't mean that all is well. There are many sensitive issues that married couples have to face that single people don't have to deal with. Of the 50 percent of marriages that fail, 80 percent of those divorced cite financial difficulties as the main cause. Truth be told, many Christian married couples fuss and fight about money a lot. Sometimes the issue is straightforward, like keeping the checkbook up to date, budgeting, or managing credit cards. Sometimes it's more complicated, like trusting your spouse with money and communication issues. Here are a few tips for keeping financial harmony at home:

Communicate with your spouse about financial issues.

Every few months or so, my wife and I go away for one full day to do nothing but plan and talk about our financial life. We share our fears, concerns, goals, accomplishments, and what we need to do to improve our finances. I believe that every couple needs to do this a few times a year. A couple needs to sit down together and develop short-range and long-range goals, such as: 1) What are we going to do about educating our children? 2) What are we going to do about retirement? 3) What would you do if I suddenly died? If you can't talk about those things, that's a sign of poor communication, and you need to deal with it.

Also, if you are engaged, please communicate your feelings and your current financial health with each other. I often recommend that engaged couples share their credit reports, the amount of debt they have, what they purchased when they went into the debt, their current incomes, their budgets, their assets and liabilities, and their financial goals. I've known a couple or two that got married, then tried to buy a house and were shocked when they were turned down by mortgage companies because one of them had bad credit. Remember, a lot of marriages end because of financial conflict. I believe in many cases the seeds of divorce are planted during the courtship and engagement period. Use this time in your relationship to deal with the real issues and not just to plan for an elaborate wedding.

Don't hide money and keep financial secrets from your spouse.

Before Martica and I got married, her mother sat her down and gave her this advice: "Always keep some money stashed away for yourself, girl—Lee doesn't have to know all your business." Now, her mother wasn't saying this because of her lack of trust or respect for me; she knew that I would take good care of her daughter. She was basically saying this because she believed that no woman should ever totally trust a man, even if they were married. Because my mother-in-law was divorced, as well as many of her friends, she believed that women, especially Black women, should always have a backup plan in case the marriage didn't work. Martica decided not to follow her mother's advice, because she felt hiding money from me would be deceitful and would undermine our marriage.

The Bible states, "A man shall leave his father and his mother, and shall cleave to his wife; and they shall become one flesh" (Genesis 2:24). Becoming "one flesh" involves two people becoming one sexually, spiritually, and financially. Keeping money secrets and separate accounts will only eat away at your marriage. It really shows that you don't trust your spouse. I believe that couples should set goals and plan their futures together. Marriage is no place for a "your money, my money" attitude but an "our" money attitude.

Agree on what the financial priorities are.

Matthew 18:19 in the *Amplified Bible* makes a powerful statement about the power of two people in agreement: "Again I tell you, if two of you on earth agree (harmonize together, together make a symphony) about—anything and everything—whatever they may ask, it will come to pass and be done for them by My Father in heaven." The point is this: When a husband and wife get on the same page, it's powerful, and they can accomplish just about anything! For my wife and me, there are different seasons in our financial life that we both have to discern and discuss. For instance, sometimes there is a season for saving money, so we both agree that saving will be a priority, so we cut back on our spending. Sometimes there's a season for spending, like buying furniture and fixing up the house. There are also seasons that we give significantly beyond our tithe. Agreeing on what season you are in and what the priorities are cut down the arguments about money.

Assess who is good at what.

I've counseled many couples that were at odds over who should keep the books and maintain the checking account. I find that with most couples I counsel that the wife, given the training, is usually the better bookkeeper. Normally she has more time and is a little more diligent. I've seen some husbands really mess things up. So here's some quick advice: I recommend that only one person should be the bookkeeper, and that person needs to keep the checkbook. If the husband needs a check (if the wife keeps the checkbook), he should borrow the checkbook, write the check, and return it that day. It is very difficult to keep your account balanced when more than one person has frequent access to the checkbook. Once you develop a workable system and determine who's good at what, then stick to it.

Make your differences count.

In marriage, oftentimes opposites attract. I believe God puts couples together to balance each other. The wife may want to invest; the husband may want to spend. The wife may like to go out to eat; the husband may like to eat in. When my wife and I got married, I was frugal, and she was carefree with money. I got my first credit card at twenty-five years old; she got her first credit card at eighteen years old (and boy, did she use it a lot!). After fourteen years of marriage, she's loosened me up some, and I've helped her gain some financial discipline. Allow your differences to complement your marriage, not to cause a war.

Finally, we must realize that what we do and who we are as married couples is multiplied many times over through our descendants. If you have two children and each of them marries and has two children, and those children in turn marry and have two children, and so forth, in only four generations, thirty families will descend from you and your spouse. If a godly heritage is passed along through those generations, what an amazing impact it can have on the world! Don't take your parenting lightly; live and leave a godly legacy.

THE JUGGLING ACT OF SINGLE PARENTS

I greatly admire and appreciate African-American single mothers and their effort to raise their children. The problem concerning many of these women is poverty due to a combination of low wages and deadbeat dads who don't pay child support. Sixty-two percent of households headed by single parents are without savings or other financial assets.[7] The problems of single moms are further complicated by a lack of low-cost, safe, reliable child-care services. Many single moms are constantly juggling bills and trying to find quality time for children between work, running errands, and household chores.

I know that life is not easy for a single parent, whether male or female. As much as we don't like to think about it, you may be just one heartbeat, one accident, away from becoming a single parent. Any of our homes could also be hit by divorce or abandonment. What I'm saying is that none of us is immune to the problems of life, so we need to know what God says about being a single parent.

First of all, let me clearly state that single parenthood in African-American families does not automatically mean that the family is dysfunctional. There are many resourceful African-American single parents with strong ties to an extended family network. Many times this extended family consists of mothers, fathers, uncles, aunts, grandparents, older brothers and sisters, neighbors, quasi-relatives, and church members. In some Black families, they all come together to meet the challenges of raising children. Oftentimes single parents are able to create stable environments for their children and do an excellent job of teaching them the skills they need to succeed in the world.

Also, many African-American single-parent families have strong ties to the church. Rather than dwell on hardships, many spiritually oriented single mothers see difficult situations as God's test of their faith, and they pray and hope for a better life for their children. In the Bible, God defends the cause of single-parent families: "He executes justice for the orphan and the widow, and shows His love for the alien by giving him food and clothing" (Deuteronomy 10:18), and He sustains the fatherless: "The Lord . . . supports the fatherless and the widow" (Psalm 146:9).

Single parents must take the pressure off themselves and realize that they can only be what God made them. No woman can be a father; no man can be a mother. A few suggestions for making single parenthood more successful are:

1. Follow the example of Joshua and serve the Lord. "But as for me and my house, we will serve the Lord" (Joshua 24:15).
2. Forgive anyone who has played a part in bringing about difficult conditions, including yourself. "But if you do not forgive others, then your Father will not forgive your transgressions" (Matthew 6:15).

3. Realistically accept the circumstances you are in, with the goal of having the best life possible. Don't become angry and bitter.

4. Get organized. Use a weekly schedule or calendar in order to have a balanced life.

5. Develop a plan for dealing with problems and making decisions. Write problems out on paper. This alone can be very helpful in seeking solutions.

6. Ask God for wisdom. "If any of you lacks wisdom, let him ask of God, who gives to all generously and without reproach, and it will be given to him" (James 1:5). Do not be led by emotions alone in decision-making. God has given some people in the body of Christ the gift of wisdom. Prayerfully ask God to lead you to them. These can be friends, relatives, or your pastor.

7. Don't share with children those burdens that are beyond their maturity or ability to understand.

8. The family should attend church regularly together. Single parents should do all they can to help their sons and daughters know Jesus Christ as their Lord and Savior.

9. Teach children how to handle money in biblical ways. Giving a child every material thing he asks for will not make up for having only one parent. Some single parents do very well as wage earners, yet they ruin their children by giving them too much.

10. Discipline your children. They must learn to obey you. They will appreciate it when they are older. Everyone in the household should share in the work required to maintain the house. Godly single parents have raised some of the most responsible children in America. So please be encouraged. I pray that the Lord will bless your efforts.

GRANDPARENTS

If you are a grandparent, you have a great opportunity to influence your grandchildren. I believe that an inheritance is more than just material possessions. A godly inheritance includes a legacy of teaching the younger generation to understand God's ways. I strongly recommend that parents meet with grandparents and together design a plan for training your children.

It is also important for grandparents to support the objectives of the parents. Some grandparents are too lenient with their grandchildren, even though they weren't like that with own their children. I'll probably be the same way with my grandchildren; I don't know. But I do know that too often parents and grandparents have not reached an agreement on how to train the next generation. This can lead to strained relationships and ineffective training for the child.

YOUR INVESTMENT IN CHILDREN

An understanding of personal finance and godly stewardship is one of the most important skills you can pass down to your children. Again, if you don't have children, you need to influence your nephews or nieces. The Bible tells us to care for the next generation. This idea of generation-to-generation transmission of a heritage resounds as a basic principle throughout all of Scripture. Here are just a few examples:

> "Be careful, and watch yourselves closely so that you do not forget the things your eyes have seen or let them slip from your heart as long as you live. Teach them to your children and to their children after them." (Deuteronomy 4:9 NIV)

> "Tell ye your children of it, and let your children tell their children, and their children another generation." (Joel 1:3 KJV)

> "What we have heard and known, what our fathers have told us. We will not hide them from their children; we will tell the next generation the praiseworthy deeds of the LORD, his power, and the wonders he has done. He decreed statutes for Jacob and established the law in Israel, which he commanded our forefathers to teach their children, so the next generation would know them, even the children yet to be born, and they in turn would tell their children. Then they would put their trust in God and would not forget his deeds but would keep his commands." (Psalm 78:3–7 NIV)

As you can see, remembering the blessings of the Lord and con-veying them to the next generation is a constant theme in the Bible. But how do we practically do this? How do we position ourselves to make an impact on a child's life? When you left home, how well pre-pared were you to make financial decisions? Parents and teachers spend generally less than a few hours teaching the value and use of the mon-ey children will earn during their careers. Here are three methods you can use to teach biblical principles to children.

1. Verbally communicate.

The Lord charged the Israelites, "These words, which I am com-manding you today, shall be on your heart. You shall teach them dili-gently to your sons and shall talk of them when you sit in your house and when you walk by the way and when you lie down and when you rise up" (Deuteronomy 6:6–7). We must verbally instruct our children in the ways of the Lord, but children need more than verbal instruction; they also need a good example.

2. Be a godly model.

It's really hard to fool kids. They see through things so quickly. Every parent knows what it's like to be confronted with the simple but penetrating analysis of a child who has identified a fine point of hypocrisy.

Before going to speak at a Promise Keepers Men's Conference a few years ago, I promised my daughter that I would take her skating when I got back in town. After I returned home, I didn't feel up to going, be-cause I was exhausted from the trip. I tried to explain that to my daugh-ter, but she looked at me and said, "Dad, I thought you were a promise keeper." Needless to say, I took her skating that night.

Regardless of what you say to your kids and grandchildren, what they're going to remember is what you do. Children soak up parental attitudes toward money like a sponge soaks up water. Most children gen-erally follow their parents' lead when it comes to money habits. If your purchases are driven by conspicuous consumption, then their purchases will be driven by a psychological need to keep up with the Joneses, too.

Paul recognized the importance of example when he said, "Be imitators of me, just as I also am of Christ" (1 Corinthians 11:1). The Lord used both of these techniques. He gave us His written Word, the Bible, and also sent the perfect model, Jesus Christ, to demonstrate how we should live. Luke 6:40 is a challenging passage. It reads, "Everyone, after he has been fully trained, will be like his teacher." Another way of saying this is that we can teach what we believe, but we only reproduce who we are. We must be good models.

3. Give them practical experience.

Children then need to be given opportunities to apply what they have heard and seen. The two experiences which will benefit the child the most are teaching them how to spend wisely (money management) and teaching them the value of work (moneymaking).

LEARNING EXPERIENCES:
MONEY MANAGEMENT FOR CHILDREN

Learning to handle money should be part of a child's education. This is a part that the parents must direct themselves and not delegate to teachers. Consider letting your children experience these five areas as soon as possible:

1. Allow the child to earn an income.

As soon as the child is ready for school, he should begin to receive an income to manage. Parents need to decide whether the child must earn the income or if they wish to give an allowance. The amount of the income will vary according to the child's age and the financial circumstances of the family. However, the amount of the income is not as important as the responsibility of handling money.

At first, it is a new experience, and the child will make many mistakes. Do not hesitate to let the "law of natural consequences" run its course. You are going to be tempted to help little Johnny when he spends all the income the first day on an unwise purchase. But do not bail him out! His mistakes will be his best teacher. Parents should establish boundaries and offer advice on how to spend money, but your child must have the freedom of choice within those boundaries. Excessive restrictions will only reduce opportunities to learn. The first few pennies will make a lasting impression.

My wife and I bought one of our sons a new set of drums a few years ago, and he tore it up within the first few weeks. For months he begged us to buy him a new set, but we told him no, he would have to save his own money and buy his own. After a year, he saved enough money to finally buy the set. He didn't treat the new drums the way he treated the set his mother and I bought for him. Because he had his own money invested in the set, he wanted to make sure he took good care of it.

2. Teach your children how to budget.

When children start to receive an income, teach them how to budget. Begin with a simple system consisting of three boxes or jars, each labeled separately—share, save, and spend. The child distributes a portion of his income into each box. Thus a simple budget is established by using visual control. Even a six year old can understand this method, because when there is no more money to spend, the box is empty!

As the child matures, he should participate in the family budget. It will help him understand the limitations of income and how to stretch the money to meet needs.

When the child becomes a teenager, he or she should begin a written budget.

During the budget training, teach your child to become a wise consumer. Teach shopping skills, the ability to distinguish needs from wants, and the importance of waiting on the Lord to provide.

3. Get your children saving for the future.

The habit of saving should be established as soon as the child receives an income. It is helpful to open a savings account for the child at this time. Teach your children the benefits of compounding interest. If they grasp this concept and become faithful savers, they will enjoy financial stability as adults. Parents should demonstrate this principle by saving for something that will directly affect and benefit the children, such as a vacation. Use a graph the children can fill in so they can visually chart the progress of saving.

Children should have both short-term and long-term saving programs. The younger the child, the more important short-term goals are. To a four year old, a week seems like a lifetime to save for a small purchase. He will not understand saving for his future education but will get excited about saving for a small toy. Long-term saving, such as for education and a first car, should be a requirement. Some parents find it motivating to their child if they match some of their child's contribution to their long-term savings.

4. Teach children about debt.

It is also important to teach the cost of money and how difficult it is to get out of debt. A father loaned his son and daughter the money to buy bicycles. He drew up a credit agreement with a schedule for repayment of the loan, including the interest charged. After they went through the long, difficult process of paying off the loan, the family celebrated with a "mortgage-burning" ceremony. The father said that his children appreciated those bikes more than any of their other possessions and vowed to avoid debt in the future.

5. Get children in the habit of giving.

The best time to establish the habit of giving is when a child is young. It is helpful for children to give a portion of their gifts to a real need they can see. For example, a child understands the impact of his gift when his contribution is helping to build the church he can see under construction or buying food or clothing for a family that has greater needs than he does. We also recommend a time each week for dedicating that week's gifts to the Lord. It is important for the children to participate in this time of dedication and worship. The more involvement children have in the proper handling of money, the better habits they will have as adults.

LEARNING EXPERIENCES :
MONEYMAKING FOR CHILDREN

Parents also have the responsibility to train children in the value of work and in the development of proper work habits. If the child responds and learns how to work with the proper attitude, he or she will become a valuable commodity in the job market. Good employees are difficult to find. Clearly, children need to learn the dignity and habit of work. There are four areas to consider in this training:

Learning routine responsibilities

The best way for a child to become faithful in work is to establish the habit of daily household chores. These are chores that each member of the family is expected to perform. For example, one of my sons carries out the garbage, the other washes the dishes, and my daughter cleans the floors.

Exposing children to different kinds of work

Many children do not know how their father or mother earn income or the many different types of jobs that are available. An important way to teach the value of work is to expose the child to the parents' means of making a living. If your children cannot visit you at work, at least take the time to explain your job to them. For parents who manage their own business, children should be encouraged to participate. Additionally, speak with teachers, guidance counselors, and members of your church about opportunities for your child to learn about their jobs and how they went about preparing themselves and getting their jobs.

Working for others

Baby-sitting, bagging groceries, or waiting on tables will be an education. A job gives a child an opportunity to enter into an employee-employer relationship and to earn extra money.

The objective of training your child in the value of work is to build and discipline his or her character. A working child with the proper attitude will be a more satisfied individual. He or she will grow up with more respect for the value of money and the effort required to earn it.

Dependency on prayer

One of the most valuable lessons you can teach your children is to seek the Lord's guidance and His provision through prayer. The Lord wants to show us that He is alive and actively involved in our lives. One way He does this is by answering our prayers. We often rob ourselves of this opportunity by buying things or charging purchases without praying that the Lord would supply them.

Danger of television

Television has affected children and their values in ways we have not yet begun to understand. Consider these statistics: By the time the typical teenager graduates from high school, he has spent 10,800 hours in class and 15,000 hours in front of the "tube." Children spend more time watching television (30 to 50 hours per week) than any other activity except sleeping, and they will see approximately one million commercials by age twenty. A recent survey asked children if they would rather give up television or their fathers—44 percent said they would forsake their fathers.

The influence of television on children is so potentially dangerous that parents cannot afford to ignore it. Rather, they must carefully control the programs their children watch.

LEAVING AN INHERITANCE

Parents should attempt to leave a material inheritance to their children. "A good man leaves an inheritance to his children's children" (Proverbs 13:22). The inheritance should not be given until the child has been trained to be a wise steward. "An inheritance gained hurriedly at the beginning will not be blessed in the end" (Proverbs 20:21). In my opinion, you should make provision in your will for distributing an inheritance over several years or until the heir is mature enough to handle the responsibility of money. Select those you trust to supervise the youth until he is a capable steward.

MAKE SURE YOU HAVE A WILL

It is important to prepare financially for your death. As Isaiah told Hezekiah, "Thus says the Lord, 'Set your house in order, for you shall die'" (2 Kings 20:1). Someday, if the Lord does not return first, you will die. If you do not have a current will or trust, the government and not you will determine how the fruit of your labor is going to be divided among your heirs. Only 20 percent of African-Americans develop a will.[8]

Some Black folks believe that talking about death and planning for it somehow speeds up that inevitable moment. So instead of planning, we do nothing. After we die, we let our family members fight and fuss over our stuff. Why not spare your family from all the bickering by doing some simple pre-death planning?

One of the greatest gifts you can leave your family for that emotional time will be an organized estate and a properly prepared will or revocable living trust.

Chapter Eleven

LEAVING A LASTING FINANCIAL LEGACY

Tyrone and April were students in my financial class and were quite financially astute. They lived within their means, lived on a budget, gave to God's work, and saved consistently. As a matter of fact, they knew as much about stewardship and money-management issues as I did. They were two of my best students, and they seemed to soak in everything I was saying. They had two beautiful young children, ages one and three. They owned an inexpensive car and had just bought their first home. They also had two insurance policies for $100,000, one on each spouse's life.

They came to my office to talk to me about a serious disagreement they were having as a couple that involved finances. I was shocked, because they always seemed to agree on everything, especially when it came to money.

The disagreement started when Tyrone and April began discussing what would happen if they both died together. They discussed who would be the best person to raise their kids and manage the insurance money.

April said her sister Susan would be the wisest choice, because she was securely married with one child of her own. Tyrone didn't think that was a wise choice, because Susan's husband did not know the Lord, and Tyrone wanted his kids to always be in a strong Christian home. Tyrone suggested that his mother would be the ideal choice, because she obviously did a good job raising him, and she could do the same for her grandchildren, if she had to. April adamantly disagreed. "Tyrone, your mother is too old to raise young children," she said. "Furthermore, she has a bad temper," Susan added. That didn't set too well with Tyrone.

They came to me to talk out some of these issues and were able to resolve their conflict. However, after they left my office, I realized that I had not thought through my own situation. Who would care for my children should Martica and I go to meet God together? I really didn't want to think about it, but I knew this was some business I had to take care of.

FEAR OF THE UNKNOWN

There is a story of a businessman who traveled with his boss to New York City. Early one morning, milling through the marketplace, the businessman sees Death in human form. Death gives him a threatening look, and the businessman recoils in terror, convinced that Death intends to take him that day.

The businessman runs to his boss and says, "Mr. Boss, help me. I have seen Death, and his threatening look tells me he intends to take my life this very day. I must escape him. Please let me leave now and catch the next plane to Chicago where Death cannot find me." His boss agrees, and the terrified businessman is off quickly on the next flight to Chicago.

A few hours later, the boss himself sees Death among the crowded streets of New York City. He boldly approaches Death and asks him, "Why did you give the businessman who works for me that threatening look today?"

"That was not a threatening look," Death replies. "That was a look of surprise. You see, I was amazed to see him in New York City, for I have an appointment with him tonight in Chicago."

The moral of this story is best summed up by Randy Alcorn in his masterful and profound book *Money, Possessions, and Eternity:* "The time of our death is unknown. The way of our death is unpredictable. The fact of our death is inescapable."

The thought of death just terrifies some people, but even so, you need to be prepared for it spiritually and financially. First, let me ask you this: What are the odds that you will die someday? Last time I looked, the odds weren't in your favor, or mine. Hebrews 9:27 says, "It is appointed for men to die once and after this comes judgment."

See, you and I have an appointment to die. And, lest you think you can somehow get out of it, I want you to know this: We may be late for a lot of things in life, but this is one appointment we're not going to miss. In fact, we're going to be right on time.

Death is a fact of life. It's a sure thing. We may spend our lives running from death and denying death, but that won't stop it from coming at its appointed time. The problem is, we don't know when it's going to happen. And I think that adds to our anxiety about death and the afterlife. Some people even get so anxious that they refuse to think about it. But ignoring the inevitable does not make it go away.

In the African-American culture there is a lot of fear surrounding death. Most people I know, even in my own family, dislike talking about it or anything associated with it. Some people think that if they discuss and make plans for their death, then that will make it happen sooner. So they put off planning (as if that postpones it), and when they finally die, family members are left fussing and fighting over belongings because the deceased didn't take care of his business. Not talking about death won't postpone it, and talking about it won't bring it any sooner.

ESTATE PLANNING

It is not only prudent but necessary for African-American households to discuss what to do after a family member passes away. This is called estate planning and essentially means deciding who gets your property after you die, then choosing the wisest legal transfer method, or methods, for leaving your property to those you want to receive it.

Your "plan" when completed will simply be the documents necessary to carry out your basic decisions. Don't think you have to map out some grand strategy. Many estate plans are quite simple and easy to create.

The most important part of planning your estate is deciding who will get your property after you die, and, if you have minor children, who should care for them if you cannot. Other examples of issues people face are: How will creditors be paid after the breadwinner dies? Will the kids be able to attend college? Who will inherit the deceased's assets? How much money will the deceased's survivors need? As you can see, these are personal decisions, certainly not matters for lawyers or other "experts" to figure out for you. You have to really seek the Lord's guidance, because many of these decisions will have generational repercussions.

As you can see, your financial responsibilities do not expire when you do. When it comes to planning for your investments, time is your best friend. But when it comes to planning for death and leaving a legacy, time can be your worst enemy. You must start getting your financial house in order while you are still alive, so other people won't have to make decisions for you after your passing. Whether you are married or single, you have to love your family enough to prepare them for your departure and to help ensure their financial welfare.

INSURING YOUR FUTURE

Investing is for opportunity. Insurance is for the unknown. Investing is about taking risks. Insurance is about eliminating risks. Not having adequate insurance is like playing football without pads. When you get tackled, it's going to hurt real badly. In football, you may not be able to eliminate being tackled by three-hundred-pound linebackers, but you can decide to protect yourself when they come your way.

Insurance is a guarantee against loss. By purchasing an insurance contract or policy, the purchaser is assured of recovering from a large loss should it occur. Both possessions and people can be insured. You can insure your home, your paycheck, your health, your business—even your life. As Christians, we should all expect the best but be prepared for the worst.

Life insurance

Life insurance has been around since the days of the early Roman Empire, when the legionnaires pledged a portion of their pay to a fund for the families of the soldiers who did not survive the various wars. Even though insurance has become more complicated and confusing in the last two thousand years, it's still used primarily for the same purposes.

Life insurance is really death insurance, because it is payable upon a person's death. Regardless of what you may read or what agents may tell you, the only reason to buy life insurance is to meet your obligations to your family in the event of your death. Life insurance is not a good savings plan or a good investment. There are far better investment choices than an insurance policy to meet your financial goals.

Based on my fifteen years' experience in the financial services profession, insurance is the last thing most African-Americans buy when they have money, and the first thing they drop when things get tight financially.

I know a young lady that went through a tragic experience recently. Her husband died suddenly of a heart attack, and, unfortunately, he didn't have any life insurance. I couldn't believe that this outstanding man of God didn't at least have a small policy on himself. Well, I found out that he did have life insurance at one time, but when finances got tight, he and his wife stopped paying the insurance premium and let the policy lapse. One month later he died. Look here: Even if you have to get your cable TV service or cell phone cut off, please make sure you keep adequate life insurance on yourself. Don't put your family at risk.

Although I think insurance is good, something is terribly wrong when a man's most effective avenue of material provision for his family is his own death. A lot of adults in the Black community are worth a whole lot more dead than alive, financially speaking. I don't know about you, but I want to be able to see my children's faces and my wife's face as I bless them financially. I don't want to just bless them at the coffin, but I want to bless them at the coffee table too. Think about it. Will most of the financial legacy you leave to the next generation be at the coffin or the coffee table?

One controversial issue about life insurance is this debate between whole life and term insurance. There is also a hybrid of the two called universal life. Simply put, term insurance is purely death coverage. There is no savings component, and the premiums increase with your age. It's also cheap. If you have term insurance, you are basically renting. With whole life insurance, the premiums are higher at the beginning to compensate for when you get older. Also, there is a savings component offering a small interest rate. Whole life insurance is similar to buying instead of renting, because you can accumulate cash value or equity in the policy. I personally prefer term instead of whole life, because the higher premiums I would pay for the whole life policy I can invest to build my estate. I have known of many cases where whole life was appropriate, though. My point is not to argue which is better. All financial-planning decisions have to be based on what is best for each individual. There is no cookie-cutter approach to insurance or investing.

How much insurance do you need?

All the formulas about how much insurance you need don't work perfectly for everyone. The average policy sale is $100,000, which isn't nearly enough for a young family with a mortgage, children, and credit-card bills. After burial expenses of about $5,000, you'll need enough to take care of mortgage payments, a car note, the normal cost of rearing your children, their medical and dental bills, and future tuition.

According to Brooke Stephens, author of *Wealth Happens One Day at a Time,* the average family breadwinner needs at least $500,000 in life insurance protection to replace his or her paycheck for at least ten years. In the event of death, this money should be moved into some income-producing investments that would provide at least $40,000 to $50,000 a year. Stephens goes on to say that you should take a look at your total savings, retirement plan, private insurance, and group life coverage available through your employer to determine how many years' income could be replaced by those total assets. Each person's needs are as different as his or her fingerprints. The real answer depends on your financial profile:

- Your yearly income and how many years are left until the children are out of the house
- The standard of living the family will want to maintain if you were absent
- The amount of debts that needs to be paid off

One last thing about insurance: Whether you are married with children or single with no dependents, you should have an adequate health policy and a very strong disability policy. If you ever have an accident or long-term illness, the bills don't stop when you're incapacitated. Disability insurance replaces up to 70 percent of your income if you're ill or injured for a lengthy period.

WHERE THERE'S A WILL, THERE'S A WAY

Roughly seven out of ten Americans die without wills. Between 200,000 and 250,000 Americans under the age of forty-five die unexpectedly each year. Think of what that means. To die without a will is expensive and time-consuming and can be heartbreaking for your loved ones. It can literally destroy an estate left to provide for the family.

Only 20 percent of African-Americans have a will. If we want to leave a legacy to our children, then we must design wills and trusts that clearly explain how the fruits of our labor are going to be divided.

Scripture teaches that we brought nothing into the world, and we will take nothing with us when we die, but we can leave it precisely as we wish. We can stipulate to whom and how much. If you die without a will, these decisions are left up to the court. Under some circumstances, the court can appoint a guardian to raise your children if you have not made this provision in your will.

Whether you are married or single, rich or poor, you should have a will. Not only does it clear up any legal uncertainties, but it also helps you map out your finances while you are alive so that you can protect the best interest of your heirs.

About thirty-six out of one hundred people die before retirement age. So do not put off preparation of your will just because you are young. Do it now! As Isaiah told Hezekiah, "Thus says the Lord, 'Set your house in order, for you shall die" (2 Kings 20:1). One of the greatest gifts you can leave your family for that emotional time will be an organized estate and current will or trust. Please make an appointment with an attorney to prepare one.

LEAVING AN INHERITANCE

As I said in the previous chapter, I believe that parents should attempt to leave an inheritance to their children. According to Proverbs 13:22, "A good man leaves an inheritance to his children's children." The inheritance should not be dispensed until the child has been thoroughly trained to be a wise steward. "An inheritance gained hurriedly at the beginning will not be blessed in the end" (Proverbs 20:21).

The parable of the prodigal son is a perfect example of what can happen to a person who gets an inheritance before he has the ability to handle it. My mother always used to tell me, "A fool and his money are soon parted." That is so true. In my opinion, you should provide for the inheritance to be distributed over several years or when the heir is mature enough to handle the responsibility of money. Select those you trust to supervise the youth until he or she is a capable steward. Galatians 4:1–2 says, "Now I say, as long as the heir is a child, . . . although he is owner of everything, but he is under guardians and managers until the date set by the father."

You should provide an inheritance for your children. However, it is probably not wise to leave your children with great wealth if they have not been thoroughly schooled in the biblical perspective of money and how to properly manage it. Andrew Carnegie once said, "The almighty dollar bequeathed to a child is an almighty curse. No one has the right to handicap his children with such a burden as great wealth. He must face this question squarely: Will the fortune be safe with my child, and will my child be safe with my fortune?"

PASSING THE BATON

The picture of a relay provides an excellent model for generational transfer. The relay only works if one person has something to pass and another person is willing to receive it. Generational transfer allows one generation to experience the blessing of "receiving the baton at full speed." Passing our faith in Christ to the next generation can also be compared to a relay race. As parents, we have the responsibility to pass the baton of practical biblical truths to our children. At times during the training, it seems as if there is little progress. but don't give up!

NOW GO AND TAKE CARE OF BUSINESS

You now know the biblical framework for managing money. But knowing is only half of the solution. You must act upon that knowledge. Jesus said,

> Everyone who hears these words of Mine and acts on them, may be compared to a wise man who built his house on the rock. And the rain fell, and the floods came, and the winds blew and slammed against that house; and yet it did not fall, for it had been founded on the rock. Everyone who hears these words of Mine and does not act on them, will be like a foolish man who built his house on the sand. The rain fell, and the floods came, and the winds blew and slammed against that house; and it fell— and great was its fall." (Matthew 7:24–27)

If you build your financial house upon solid principles found in Scripture, your house will not fall. One of the best ways to demonstrate your love for your family and future generations is to take care of your financial business. I believe God wants to raise up Christian dynasties. Will your family be one of them? It will only happen as God's people learn how to be good stewards of their financial resources. May the Lord richly bless you in every way as you draw close to Him.

LOCATION OF IMPORTANT DOCUMENTS

Date _____

Document	Location of Original	Location of Copy
Birth Certificates		
Marriage Certificate		
Military Discharge		
Wills		
Trusts		
Debt Instruments		
Power of Attorney		
Death Certificates		
Citizenship Papers		
Divorce Decree		
Deeds		
Leases		
Business Agreements		
Retirement Papers		
Automobile Titles		
Insurance Policies		
Income Tax Files		
Other Documents:		

NOTES

Introduction: Bigger and Better Dreams

1. C. Eric Lincoln and Lawrence H. Mamiya, *The Black Church in the African-American Experience* (Durham & London: Duke Univ., 1990), 241.

Chapter 1: Wealth from the Inside Out

1. Melvin L. Oliver and Thomas M. Shapiro, *Black Wealth, White Wealth: A New Perspective on Racial Equality* (New York & London: Routledge, 1995), 24, 7, 101.
2. George C. Fraser, *Race for Success: The Ten Opportunities for Blacks in America* (New York: Avon, 1998).
3. Dennis Peacocke, *Almighty and Sons: Doing Business God's Way!* (Santa Rosa: Rebuild, 1995), 59
4. Jesse Jackson Sr. and Jesse Jackson Jr. *It's About the Money* (New York: Three Rivers Press, 1999), 12.
5. Oliver and Shapiro, *Black Wealth, White Wealth*, 101.
6. Ibid., 97.
7. Beth Belton, *USA Today*.

Chapter 2: What's God Got to Do with It?

1. Melvin Oliver and Thomas Shapiro, *Black Wealth, White Wealth* (New York & London: Routledge, 1995), 37.

2. Tony Evans, *What a Way to Live: Running All of Life by the Kingdom Agenda* (Nashville: Word, 1997), 161.
3. David E. Neff, "Drunk on Money," *Christianity Today*, 8 April 1988, 15.

Chapter 3: Charting Your Financial Destiny

1. Eugene Peterson, *The Message* (Colorado Springs: NavPress, 1993), 188.
2. Eric Lincoln and Lawrence Mamiya, *The Black Church in the African-American Experience* (Durham & London: Duke Univ., 1990), 262.

Chapter 4: From Financial Bondage to Freedom

1. Kelvin Boston, *Smart Money Moves for African-Americans* (New York: Putnam, 1996), 150.

Chapter 5: Finding Purpose in Your Work

1. Story used by Dennis Kimbro, Ph.D. *What Makes the Great Great* (New York: Doubleday, 1995), 220.
2. Eric Lincoln and Lawrence Mamiya, *The Black Church in the African-American Experience* (Durham & London: Duke Univ., 1990), 237.
3. Jawanza Kunjufu, *Black Economics: Solutions for Economic and Community Empowerments* (Chicago: African-American Images,1991), 36.
4. Derek Dingle, "An Agenda for the Black Middle Class," *Black Enterprise*, November 1989, 60.

Chapter 6: Spending Your Money Wisely

1. Dennis P. Kimbro, Ph.D. *What Makes the Great Great* (New York: Doubleday, 1995), 222–23.
2. Brooke Stephens, *Talking Dollars & Making Sense: A Wealth-Building Guide for AA* (New York: McGraw Hill, 1997), 4.
3. Dennis Kimbro, *What Makes the Great Great* (New York: Doubleday, 1995), 325, and Jawanza Kunjufu, *Black Economics: Solutions for Economic and Community Empowerment* (Chicago: African-American Images, 1991), 75.
4. Kunjufu, *Black Economics*, 73.
5. Robert L. Wallace, *Black Wealth: Your Road to Small Business Success* (New York: John Wiley & Sons, 2000), 23.

Chapter 7: Giving Back to God

1. Herb Goldberg and Robert Lewis, *Money and Madness* (New York: Morrow, 1978), 13, 14.
2. F. F. Bosworth, "God's Financial Plan: Part X: Testimonies of Tithers," *Reality*, February 1981.
3. Stephen F. Olford, *The Grace of Giving: A Biblical Study of Christian Stewardship* (Grand Rapids: Kregal, 2000), 107.

NOTES

⸻ ⁓⁓ ⸻

Chapter 8: Putting Your Money to Work

1. Howard Dayton, "Crown Ministries Chronicle Newsletter," Spring 1999.
2. Angela P. Moore, "The Art of Accumulation," *Atlanta Tribune*, January 2000, 46.
3. Jawanza Kunjufu, *Black Economics: Solutions for Economic and Community Empowerment* (Chicago: African-American Images, 1991), 80.
4. Ibid., 14.
5. Ibid., 73.
6. Ibid., 114.

Chapter 10: Investing in Your Family

1. Dennis Peacocke, *Almighty & Sons: Doing Business God's Way* (Santa Rosa: Rebuild, 1995), 36.
2. Barna Research Group, *African-Americans and Their Faith: Research on the Faith, Culture, Values, and Lifestyles of Blacks in America*, The Barna Institute, 1999, 22.
3. Joseph G. Conti and Brad Stetson, *Challenging the Civil Rights Establishment: Profiles of a New Black Vanguard* (Westport & London: Praeger, 1993), 176.
4. Barna Research Group, "African-Americans and Their Faith," Internal Study 1999, 3.
5. Robert Rector interviewed by Phil Reed, "Live from LA," KKLA radio, May 21, 1992.
6. James Bock, *Baltimore Sun*, 27 June, 1997.
7. Melvin Oliver and Thomas Shapiro, *Black Wealth, White Wealth*, Routledge, 1995, 7.
8. Jawanza Kunjufu, *Black Economics: Solutions for Economic and Community Empowerment* (Chicago: African-American Images, 1991), 113.

Lift Every Voice Books

Planting Seeds of Hope
How to Reach a New Generation of African Americans with the Gospel

African American youth are looking for role models they can trust. The network of support is already in place. God has placed many of His most compassionate workers among today's African American young people. This book is written to help youth workers, pastors, parents and others who care about reaching young people with the hope of the Gospel.

ISBN#0-8024-5428-3

Flame
A Heated Romance Without Him
Burns Vigorously Out of Control

After praying that God would introduce her to a guy, Bacall meets Rory Kerry at a party. He is the student body president, the lead singer in a group called Rise, and to Bacall—perfect. Before completing her last quarter of school, her father offers her the position of Vice President of his record company and she soon realizes that the surprises and changes in her life are just beginning.

ISBN #0-8024-4197-1

God Just Showed Up

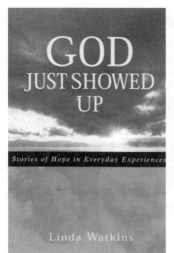

God Just Showed Up is a compilation of various short stories written by 19 talented writers and Christian educators on their personal experiences of how God changed their lives. Included is the life-story of Curtis Martin who before being known as a running back for the New York Jets football team, and the NFL 1995 Rookie of the Year, lived in fear of not reaching his 21st birthday because of the violence in his life, and how God changed his life.

ISBN#0-8024-6591-9

Sheep In Wolves Clothing
When the Actions of
a Christian Turn Criminal

Jesus warned His followers to beware of "wolves in sheep's clothing." But just as there are wolves in sheep's clothing, there are also "sheep in wolves' clothing": believers in Christ who distance themselves from their faith and walk in the ways of the world. Sheep disguised as wolves can be found almost anywhere. This powerful book is for those beloved sheep who mistakenly believe they no longer belong to the The Good Shepherd.

ISBN #0-8024-6594-3

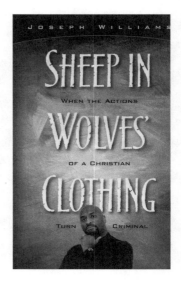